AQA
Level 3

Extended Project Qualification

Christine Andrews

HODDER
EDUCATION
AN HACHETTE UK COMPANY

Hodder Education, an Hachette UK company, Blenheim Court, George Street, Banbury, Oxfordshire OX16 5BH

Orders

Bookpoint Ltd, 130 Park Drive, Milton Park, Abingdon, Oxfordshire OX14 4SB

tel: 01235 827827

fax: 01235 400401

e-mail: education@bookpoint.co.uk

Lines are open 9:00 a.m.–5:00 p.m., Monday to Saturday, with a 24-hour message answering service. You can also order through the Hodder Education website: www.hoddereducation.co.uk

Typeset by Aptara, India

Printed in Dubai

Cover photo: Radivoje/Adobe Stock. Other photos reproduced by permission of: **p. 2** StockPhotoPro/Adobe Stock; **p. 3** Ermolaev Alexandr/Adobe Stock; **p. 5** Rawpixel.com/Adobe Stock; **p. 6** Nikolai Sorokin/Adobe Stock (*l*), donatas1205/Adobe Stock (*c*), SEF-pics/Alamy Stock Photo (*r*); **p. 12** WavebreakmediaMicro/Adobe Stock; **p. 15** aga7ta/Fotolia; **p. 16** Megan/Fotolia; **p. 17** Maxisport/Fotolia; **p. 18** Nejron Photo/Fotolia (*t*), science photo/Fotolia (*b*); **p. 22** carballo/Fotolia; **p. 23** Полина Стрелкова/Adobe Stock; **p. 25** DragonImages/Adobe Stock; **p. 26** Daniel Ernst/Adobe Stock; **p. 32** R Kawka/Alamy Stock Photo; **p. 39** Luisa Leal/Adobe Stock; **p. 40** goodluz/Adobe Stock (*t*), ShutterDivision/Adobe Stock (*b*); **p. 41** David Litschel/Alamy Stock Photo; **p.42** Graham Maddrell/Adobe Stock; **p. 43** Roberto Sorin/Adobe Stock; **p. 46** Colin Underhill/Alamy Stock Photo; **p. 47** bearsky23/Adobe Stock; **p. 48** dusanpetkovic1/Adobe Stock; **p. 50** james jagger/Alamy Stock Photo; **p. 51** Cristina Bollen/Alamy Stock Photo; **p. 54** anyaberkut/Adobe Stock; **p. 57** MShieldsPhotos/Alamy Stock Photo; **p. 58** Maurice Savage/Alamy Stock Photo; **p. 59** Tierney/Adobe Stock; **p. 61** Terry Harris/Alamy Stock Photo; **p. 63** Sergey Kamshylin/Adobe Stock; **p. 65** LittleGallery/Adobe Stock; **p. 67** anaumenko/Adobe Stock; **p. 69** LittleGallery/Adobe Stock; **p. 71** Ashok Tholpady/Alamy Stock Photo; **p. 73** Granger Historical Picture Archive/Alamy Stock Photo; **p. 76** undrey/Adobe Stock; **p. 78** Keith Tarrier/Adobe Stock; **p. 80** Monkey Business/Adobe Stock; **p. 82** undrey/Adobe Stock; **p. 84** Monkey Business/Adobe Stock; **p. 86** Granger Historical Picture Archive/Alamy Stock Photo; **p. 89** lamaip/Adobe Stock; **p. 93** kasto/Adobe Stock; **p. 94** Dmitry Vereshchagin/Adobe Stock; **p. 100** Steve Humphreys/Adobe Stock; **p. 101** Chronicle/Alamy Stock Photo; **p. 103** Phanie/Alamy Stock Photo; **p. 104** kortnyn/Adobe Stock; **p. 105** Paul Williams/Alamy Stock Photo; **p. 107** Jim West/Alamy Stock Photo; **p. 109** Moonborne/Adobe Stock; **p. 111** Lee Martin/Alamy Stock Photo; **p. 113** wjarek/Adobe Stock; **p. 115** Robert Kawka/Alamy Stock Photo; **p. 117** biker3/Adobe Stock; **p. 118** 360b/Alamy Stock Photo; **p. 119** Microgen/Adobe Stock; **p. 120** Tierney/Adobe Stock; **p. 123** Paul Doyle/Alamy Stock Photo; **p. 125** gozzoli/Adobe Stock; **p. 126** Hero Images Inc./Alamy Stock Photo; **p. 135** hjpix/Adobe Stock; **p. 136** WavebreakmediaMicro/Adobe Stock; **p. 138** jannoon128/Adobe Stock.

Hachette UK's policy is to use papers that are natural, renewable and recyclable products and made from wood grown in well-managed forests and other controlled sources. The logging and manufacturing processes are expected to conform to the environmental regulations of the country of origin.

Approval message from AQA

The core content of this textbook has been approved by AQA for use with our qualification. This means that we have checked that it broadly covers the specification and that we are satisfied with the overall quality. We do not however check or approve any links. Full details of our approval process can be found on our website.

We approve print and digital textbooks because we know how important it is for teachers and students to have the right resources to support their teaching and learning. However, the publisher is ultimately responsible for the editorial control and quality of this book.

Please note that when teaching the **AQA Extended Project Qualification** course, you must refer to AQA's specification as your definitive source of information. While this book has been written to match the specification, it cannot provide complete coverage of every aspect of the course.

A wide range of other useful resources can be found on the relevant subject pages of our website: www.aqa.org.uk.

Get the most from this book

2 Starting your project

LEARNING OUTCOMES

At the end of this chapter you should know:
- how to start the process of choosing a suitable topic for your Extended Project (EP)
- how to set yourself appropriate aims and objectives
- how to submit a good Project Proposal

Identifying possible topics

Your EP should be about a topic that interests you. Ideas for possible topics could come from something:
- that you read in a newspaper
- that was mentioned in a lesson
- related to a radio or television programme that you have heard or seen
- that you found intriguing when you undertook work experience or a research placement
- in the history, geography, geology or sociology of your home town
- unique to you and your interests

The first, and possibly hardest, part of your EPQ journey is to identify topics that you might want to examine in your EP. This might seem simple, but it requires patience and considerable effort. Do not rush into your EP with the very first idea that comes to you. Take time to consider carefully and fully the pros and cons of each idea that you have. Not all topics will result in successful EPs, even if they are of interest to you.

You should start by getting all of your initial topic ideas out of your head and down on to paper so that you can examine them. A concept map might be a good idea — or possibly several concept maps. You could use a free internet concept-mapping tool such as http://bubbl.us, or you could simply start with an A3 sheet of paper and a set of felt-tip pens.

In addition to this, it may be helpful to start a personal research journal or blog. You could use a free online blogging site such as www.blogger.com or you might use an old exercise book — the choice is yours. You can use your journal or blog to jot down any ideas or events that relate to your EP.

TIP

Keeping a research journal or blog is not essential but is highly recommended. You may use your blog or journal to help you write your Production Log, however you must **not** see your journal or blog as a substitute for the Production Log.

LEARNING OUTCOMES

Find out which skills the chapter will cover.

TIP

Get practical advice to apply to your Extended Project.

ACTIVITY

Guide your progression with activities to help you plan and implement your Extended Project.

Example

Be inspired by new ideas and ways to approach your Extended Project.

CHECKLIST

At the end of each chapter, check that you can tick off each point to succeed in your Extended Project.

ACTIVITY

Complete the tick list below to judge whether you are ready to submit your Proposal.

Topic choice:
- Am I fully committed to my chosen topic? ☐
- Will I be able to maintain interest and passion for this topic? ☐

Working title:
- Will this title help me fulfil the demands of the specification criteria? ☐
- Have I carefully considered the risks associated with this title? ☐
- Am I confident that I have a sound research base relevant to this title? ☐

Aims and objectives:
- Am I clear about what I am hoping to achieve? ☐
- Have I identified objectives that will enable me to achieve my aims? ☐

Note that at this stage you are *not* trying to formulate a title or aim; this is an initial exploration of your interests.

Example

Pardeep is exploring her interests and has come up with the following topic ideas.
- Pardeep is taking French A-level, so one possible topic could be related to the Cathar castles in the Languedoc-Roussillon region of France. This would allow her to undertake primary research in France.
- Pardeep would like to study International Relations at Higher Education (HE), so another topic could be 'The role of the UN during the Rwanda massacres'.
- Pardeep has been talking to her friends about the #MeToo social media campaign and about the celebrities who wore black at the Golden Globe awards ceremony in 2018. This might be a good topic for her to explore further.
- Her long-term aim is to go into Law, so a possible topic might be to look at whether the less well-off receive justice in equal measure to the rich.

CHECKLIST

Do I understand:
- ☐ why some topics might not be suitable for an EP?
- ☐ the difference between an aim and an objective?
- ☐ the importance of an initial resource base?
- ☐ what is required of me when I write my project proposal?
- ☐ that using a personal journal or blog will help me keep notes that can be used when I complete pages in my Log?

Contents

Chapter 9   **Submitting your work**

Appendices

Introduction

1

Why should I want to undertake the Extended Project Qualification?

Well, let's start with some reasons that might be suggested to you:

- 'It will look good on your UCAS form.'
- 'Do an EP related to one of your A-levels and you will get a better A-level grade.'
- 'Auntie Jean says you should do one because she has heard that it will make you stand out.'
- 'It looks like it will be easy, and you will get lots of free time instead of being stuck in lessons.'

Why are these reasons unsatisfactory?

Because, even though some of these suggested reasons are valid, if you do not have a genuine **interest** and **enthusiasm** for your selected EPQ topic you will not find it easy to motivate yourself or to achieve a quality outcome.

You should undertake an Extended Project if there is a topic or aspect of the world around you that you have genuine **curiosity** about and if you would like to gain the skills to allow you to satisfy this curiosity. If you decide to undertake an EP, *you* will choose the topic to be researched — a choice that will be solely owned by you.

When and if you complete your EP, you will have every right to feel proud of yourself. For this qualification, you can take all the credit. *You* will have discovered facts, ideas, techniques and opinions from different places, people and other sources. *You* will have pondered and linked those facts, ideas, techniques and opinions together, and *you* will have reached your own conclusions, some of which might be extraordinary and unexpected. No teacher will impart subject knowledge to you — you will not be expected to learn facts and regurgitate them in an examination. In this qualification, *you* are in control. *You* choose what to research, when to research, how to research, when to stop researching and what to do with your research.

Once you have completed your EP, you will have satisfied your curiosity in your chosen area of study and gained many skills that will be of great value to you in sixth form studies and higher education and in moving forward into the world of work. You will have gained confidence in your ability to solve problems, take decisions and manage your time effectively.

Students who have completed the EPQ and moved on to higher education have found it easier to bridge the gap. They have become used to independent study and being self-motivated and they have developed confidence in their own ability to succeed.

What does the EPQ involve?

Skill development

The EPQ allows you to learn and develop skills that you will apply to your own independent research project. You are expected to spend 120 hours on your EP. The EPQ is all about research and by the time you complete your project journey you should have become a confident researcher. In particular, this qualification is there for you to develop so called 'higher skills', to enable you to critically analyse your research material and draw well-judged conclusions. Do not feel anxious about your current lack of knowledge with respect to research, project management and presentation skills. Your school or college should deliver a full 30-hour programme of Taught Skills, equipping you with all the skills you will require. This Taught Skills programme will be arranged by your school's or college's EPQ centre coordinator.

You will find many suggestions and exercises within this book to help you develop and extend skills related to the EPQ.

Choice

This qualification provides you with completely free choice — you can choose to undertake a project related to *anything at all*. You will have control over your project. You will choose the project management and research skills that suit you. You will choose the project resources, you will choose your report structure and format, and you will choose the style of your presentation.

You will find many possible options related to all these choices within the chapters of this book.

Supervision

Throughout your EPQ journey you will be supervised by a member of staff from your school or college. Your supervisor, and the guidance in this book, will help you frame your research in a way that is both manageable and effective. Your supervisor will ultimately be the person who judges the quality of your project.

Product realisation

By the end of the project process you will have *either* written a 5000-word research report *or* created an artefact together with a shorter written research report (minimum 1000 words). Your report will draw carefully judged conclusions based on the research that you have undertaken (see Chapter 6). You will also have completed an AQA Production Log, providing evidence of your project 'journey'.

Presentation

You will design and deliver a live presentation to a non-specialist audience. This presentation offers you the opportunity to share your research conclusions and reflect upon the expertise that you have developed during your EPQ research journey (see Chapter 7).

Reflection

Finally, you will be expected to reflect throughout your EPQ research journey, carefully evaluating the strengths and weaknesses that you have identified in both your project and in your own learning (see Chapter 8).

Common questions about the EPQ

Why does my school/college have a centre coordinator for the EPQ?

The centre coordinator is the person who manages the delivery of the EPQ in your school or college. They will be the person who gives your proposed project formal approval, once you have convinced them that you have some good, appropriate and achievable project ideas. The coordinator allocates you to a supervisor once you have decided to embark on an EP, and the coordinator makes sure that you receive high quality teaching of skills and high-quality supervision.

What is an EPQ proposal?

Once you have thought carefully about your chosen project ideas and thoroughly discussed your plans with your supervisor, you will make a formal application to your coordinator. You will need to provide a working title, but this may well be refined once your research gets underway. You will also need to provide clear aims and objectives related to this working title. You will identify all the relevant sources that you have already found and you will need to convince the coordinator that your chosen topic does not overlap with other Level 3 studies you are undertaking (you cannot get something for nothing — an EPQ topic must extend and develop your studies).

Chapter 2 provides you with plenty of ideas and suggestions to consider as you begin to formulate your initial ideas.

5

What is an EPQ 'product'?

It will be useful for you to understand the vocabulary used by the exam board. The word '**project**' refers to the whole EPQ research journey. This includes your choice of topic, your aims and objectives, the research undertaken, the arguments presented and the conclusions reached in your written report, your EPQ presentation and your evaluation throughout the project process.

The word '**product**' refers to that which you choose to realise, following your research. Your product may be a 5000-word research report (similar, perhaps, to a university-style dissertation) or it may be an artefact of some sort, together with a shorter research report (of at least 1000 words).

What is the difference between an artefact and non-artefact project?

You may choose as your product to write a 5000-word report. Alternatively, you may choose to use your research to inform design decisions related to something that you wish to create. In this case, your product will be an artefact. Please note, however, that choosing to produce an artefact is not an 'easier' option. An artefact must have an intended user or a target audience, and in your project planning you should include the means by which you can test your planned artefact for its fitness for purpose.

Examples of artefacts include:

- some form of creative writing
- a performance
- an event
- a computer program
- a film
- a musical composition
- a website
- a game
- a piece of furniture
- a garden design
- a piece of sculpture
- a piece of jewellery
- a lesson
- an experiment

This list gives *just a few* possible artefacts. Potential artefacts are limited only by what can be achieved in the time available, with the resources that you have access to, and, of course, by your imagination.

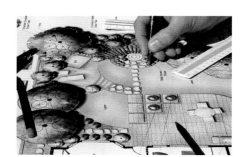

Both artefact and non-artefact products are realised as the result of research. For any Extended Project, you will need to develop appropriate skills and undertake relevant research.

If you choose to produce an artefact, you will be required also to write a research report. This report accompanies your artefact, and it should be fully referenced and written in formal academic language. It should be of minimum length 1000 words and should detail exactly how the research that you have undertaken has influenced the design decisions taken by you. Skills related to accurate referencing and use of bibliography will be required for this report just as much as if you choose to write a 5000-word report as your product. Do not worry if you have not yet learned how to write a formal referenced report. You will receive teaching for all of the required skills.

Table 1.1 What is the difference between an artefact and a 5000-word report?

Question	5000-word report as product	Artefact plus shorter report as product
Do I have a supervisor?	Yes	Yes
Can I work as a member of a group?	No	Yes
Will I complete an AQA Production Log?	Yes	Yes
How long will my report be?	5000 words	1000–5000 words
Do I need to do research?	Yes	Yes, all your design decisions should be influenced by research
Should I seek a conclusion?	Yes, your conclusion should be based on the evidence gathered during your research	Yes, this will relate to your artefact: Does it work? Is it fit for purpose? What feedback have you received?
Should my report be referenced?	Yes	Yes
How long will I spend on my project?	Minimum 90 hours	Minimum 90 hours
Should I produce a bibliography?	Yes	Yes
Should my artefact have a purpose/ intended user?	N/A	Yes

TIP

If you are considering working with others in a group, think carefully about the risks involved. How will you cope if one group member is taken ill or gives up their role within the group for other reasons? Have you considered the group dynamic, are you all equally committed and enthusiastic? (See Chapter 8.)

TIP

While most schools and colleges will have decided when projects must be finally submitted, there should be nothing to stop you managing the timings of your own project. You should be setting yourself deadlines, not expecting to be given them all.

Chapter 4 provides ideas to consider when selecting your sources, as well as other research skills. Chapter 6 includes help with bibliography and referencing.

Do I have to undertake my project alone?

It is possible to work as a member of a group when undertaking the EPQ. For some artefacts, the scope of the intended product is simply too large for one person, for example putting on a large fashion show or raising money for a specified charity. Provided that the tasks associated with the event are divided up evenly and provided that each task involves suitable research undertaken at an appropriate level, such artefacts could be suitable as a group project. Each member of the group will be judged separately, they will submit individual and unique Production Logs and reports, and they will each create a separate presentation. Only the final artefact is common to the members of the group. Members of a group may all share the same supervisor, but it is equally likely that each member of the group will have a different supervisor.

You can find guidance relating to working as a member of a group in Chapter 2.

How long will it take me to complete my project?

Your coordinator will decide when you will start your project and when you will submit your completed project. Between those two dates you should spend a minimum of 30 hours learning skills via your school's or college's Taught Skills programme and at least 90 hours applying

TIP

Remember that you will be expected to spend at least 90 hours working independently on your project, in addition to the 30 hours of skills teaching that you will receive.

TIP

The judgement of your EP does *not* just focus on the quality of your completed product. Always keep this in mind.

TIP

When writing your Log, tell the reader **why** you have taken various decisions. Do not just tell them **what** you have done or are going to do. Do *not* regard your Log as merely a document in which to record time management.

these skills to your own independent project. You will have to manage and use your own time, as most EPQ work is undertaken outside formal lesson time.

How will my Extended Project be judged?

The judgement of the quality of your EP is based entirely on the evidence that has been submitted by you. There *must* be:

- a fully completed Production Log
- a research report
- an account of your presentation

There *might* also be some additional evidence, such as photographs, video, relevant appendices (this varies from project to project).

Your project will be judged by your supervisor at the end of the EPQ process, via the four sets of AQA criteria shown in Appendix 5. It is a good idea to read these criteria. You will see that they relate to your decision-making, your selection of suitable resources and your use of these resources as you realise your chosen product.

Chapter 9 provides suggestions for you to consider as you prepare to submit your completed project to your supervisor.

The EPQ is a process-based qualification. It is *not* testing knowledge recall. Judgement of your EP includes:

- Your choice of topic — was it appropriate, did it encourage analysis?
- Your final title — did it seek an evidence-based conclusion?
- Your evidenced project planning and management.
- Your evidenced selection, evaluation and critical analysis of sources.
- Your evidenced decisions that led to the developments and changes made as your project progressed.
- Your communication, both oral at your presentation and written within your research report.
- Your conclusions drawn from your research evidence.
- Your evaluation of the completed project.
- The evaluation that you make relating to your own learning.

Why do I have an EPQ Production Log?

One of the key skills that you will be developing as you undertake your EPQ is that of project management. The Log is the document in which you plot the progress of your entire EPQ research journey. It is a working document. You can use bullet points, diagrams — whatever suits you and your personal style. Each page in the Log is completed at a certain stage in your project journey. The Log should be detailed and reflective so that anyone reading it can clearly follow your journey and understand how research has dictated the decisions you have taken.

The figure on page 9 provides an overview of the EPQ process you will be following once you have decided to undertake the EPQ, and links it to the sections within your Log. Timings are flexible and will, at least in part, be determined by your school's or college's centre coordinator.

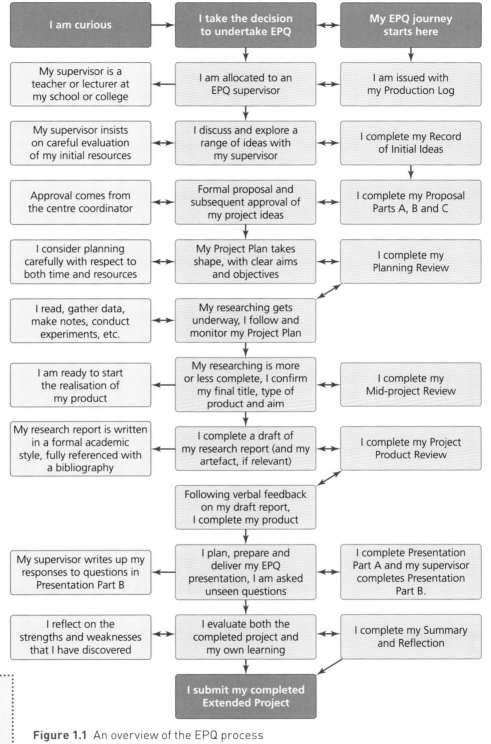

Figure 1.1 An overview of the EPQ process

What does 'independent working' mean?

No one should be taking decisions for you while you undertake your project. You should make all the decisions yourself — what to research, how to research, when and where the research is undertaken, how to use and analyse your research. This is what is meant by 'working independently'.

You will plan how to spend your time, what to do, where to go, what to read, who to interview, etc. But this does not mean that you have to work alone. You can seek advice, particularly from your supervisor, but the decisions about how to act should all come from you. This is *your* project.

It is possible to seek out a specialist mentor as part of your research. For example, this could be an expert in your chosen field of research or someone with the technical skills you need to learn. If this is a route that you choose, keep careful records of all meetings with your mentor and provide transcripts of any interviews that take place. You should treat a mentor in the same way as a book or online article: as a source of information that requires careful critical analysis. Chapter 4 provides guidance related to the use of people as sources within your research.

How do I make the best 'use' of my EPQ supervisor?

It is important to understand that an EPQ supervisor is not expected to have *any* subject knowledge related to your chosen EP topic. What they should have, though, is experience and wisdom. You would be well advised to make use of both of these qualities. You should expect your supervisor to be asking you 'Why…?' For example:

- 'Why is this book a good resource for you to use?'
- 'Why are you structuring your report like this?'
- 'Why have you not included the data from 1999?'

It may be the case that you will have regular timetabled meetings with your supervisor. If this is not the case then you will need to establish a regular agreed meeting time and place. You will also need to establish interactive channels of communication. For example, the use of blogs is becoming very popular with EPQ students. Whatever forms of communication you set up need to be established at the outset, along with other organisational issues. For example, will your supervisor be able to answer questions via e-mail? Does your supervisor have a drop-in office hour?

You are allowed to show your supervisor drafts of your work as it progresses but your supervisor is *not* allowed to annotate or mark these drafts. Any feedback that you receive from your supervisor should be general, non-directive and verbal.

Why do I have to attend Taught Skills lessons?

If you choose not to attend or engage with Taught Skills lessons it is unlikely that you will be able to demonstrate, in your completed project submission, the skills expected by the qualification. The EPQ is all about skill development and the decisions you make about how and when these skills are utilised effectively. You are not expected to start the qualification with these skills already developed. Through your school's or college's Taught Skills programme you will be taught the following:

- Different project management methods to enable you to choose the methods that suit *you*.
- Vital research skills that will enable you to choose and evaluate relevant resources suitable for *your* project, including safe use of the internet and effective use of libraries.
- How to make the best possible use of your resources and how to avoid plagiarism.

TIP

To make the best 'use' of your supervisor, ask them to be critical. Ask your supervisor questions: Is my argument logical? Do you think I have included enough case studies? How important do you think it is for me to find an academic with a different opinion? But do *not* ask them to take decisions for you.

TIP

As each skill is taught, think carefully about how it might be used to aid your project process and outcome. But remember, not all skills will be appropriate to your project, and you do not *have* to use any particular skills. Evidence of choices made by you will demonstrate that you have taken your own decisions.

- A range of skills related to the presentation of your evidence, including how to write an academic research report and how to reference the ideas that are included in your report.
- Oral presentation techniques, in particular how to communicate effectively with a non-specialist audience.
- How to reflect on your learning and judge the quality of your project journey.

For some students, when appropriate, there will be additional teaching. For example, teaching related to health and safety and risk assessment, or teaching related to the ethics of research involving human beings or animals (see Appendices 1 and 2). It will be up to you to develop these skills in order to select and use those that work best for you and your project.

You will find plenty of suggestions relating to skills development within the chapters of this book.

How does the EPQ fit in alongside my other studies?

The EPQ should complement your other Level 3 studies. The transferable skills you learn for the EPQ are relevant to any independent research activities you may undertake. Many universities now value the EPQ highly and include it in their UCAS offers. In terms of UCAS currency, the EPQ is worth half of a full A-level (e.g. an A* EPQ will gain you 28 UCAS points).

Here are just a few citations taken from university websites:

> *The University of Southampton believes the EPQ offers an unparalleled introduction to the skills needed for students to thrive in higher education.*

From the University of Oxford:

> *Working on an EPQ encourages students to develop research and academic skills relevant to undergraduate study.*

From the University of East Anglia:

> *Completing an Extended Project Qualification (EPQ) is great preparation for studying at university.*

CHECKLIST

Questions that I need to consider:

☐ Do I have time, or can I make time, to undertake an EP alongside my other sixth-form studies and activities?

☐ Is there a question, concern or area of interest I feel curious about? Does this curiosity have appropriate Level 3 scope?

☐ How likely is it that resources related to the object of my curiosity will be accessible to me?

☐ Do I understand that success in this qualification depends largely on my self-motivation and that my supervisor is not there to take decisions for me?

☐ Do I understand that judgement of my EP will be based on evidence submitted by me and that the responsibility for submission of this evidence will be entirely my own?

2 Starting your project

LEARNING OUTCOMES

At the end of this chapter you should know:

- how to start the process of choosing a suitable topic for your Extended Project (EP)
- how to set yourself appropriate aims and objectives
- how to submit a good Project Proposal

TIP

Keeping a research journal or blog is not essential but is highly recommended. You may use your blog or journal to help you write your Production Log, however you must **not** see your journal or blog as a substitute for the Production Log.

Identifying possible topics

Your EP should be about a topic that interests you. Ideas for possible topics could come from something:

- that you read in a newspaper
- that was mentioned in a lesson
- related to a radio or television programme that you have heard or seen
- that you found intriguing when you undertook work experience or a research placement
- in the history, geography, geology or sociology of your home town
- unique to you and your interests

The first, and possibly hardest, part of your EPQ journey is to identify topics that you might want to examine in your EP. This might seem simple, but it requires patience and considerable effort. Do not rush into your EP with the very first idea that comes to you. Take time to consider carefully and fully the pros and cons of each idea that you have. Not all topics will result in successful EPs, even if they are of interest to you.

You should start by getting all of your initial topic ideas out of your head and down on to paper so that you can examine them. A concept map might be a good idea — or possibly several concept maps. You could use a free internet concept-mapping tool such as http://bubbl.us, or you could simply start with an A3 sheet of paper and a set of felt-tip pens.

In addition to this, it may be helpful to start a personal research journal or blog. You could use a free online blogging site such as www.blogger.com or you might use an old exercise book — the choice is yours. You can use your journal or blog to jot down any ideas or events that relate to your EP.

ACTIVITY

Write down at least one topic from a minimum of three of the following areas:

- A topic that interests you that is directly related to your A-levels or other Level 3 study.
- A topic related to your preferred higher education course.
- A topic you have been discussing with your friends or family.
- A topic related to your long-term career aspirations.
- A topic related to a work experience or summer study programme that you have attended.
- A topic that is frequently in the news.
- A topic that allows you to maintain an interest in a subject you no longer study but previously enjoyed.
- A topic related to a special interest of yours.

Note that at this stage you are *not* trying to formulate a title or aim; this is an initial exploration of your interests.

 Example

Pardeep is exploring her interests and has come up with the following topic ideas.

- Pardeep is taking French A-level, so one possible topic could be related to the Cathar castles in the Languedoc-Roussillon region of France. This would allow her to undertake primary research in France.
- Pardeep would like to study International Relations at Higher Education (HE), so another topic could be 'The role of the UN during the Rwanda massacres'.
- Pardeep has been talking to her friends about the #MeToo social media campaign and about the celebrities who wore black at the Golden Globe awards ceremony in 2018. This might be a good topic for her to explore further.
- Her long-term aim is to go into Law, so a possible topic might be to look at whether the less well-off receive justice in equal measure to the rich.
- Pardeep undertook work experience at a local charity recently and became very interested in fundraising. Possibly this would make a good topic for her EP.
- Brexit is a recurring news topic; this could be a subject for Pardeep's EP.
- When Pardeep selected her A-levels she gave up all her creative options. She could choose an EP topic that allows her to create something.
- Pardeep has read in the literature from her chosen HE institution that she will be expected to undertake group work. Pardeep could use the opportunity to work as part of a group for her EP and produce something with another student or with a group of students.

Pardeep starts a concept map, using these ideas (Figure 2.1).

ACTIVITY

Create a concept map for *your* EP ideas. Start with the topics that you identified in the previous activity and let your ideas travel in any direction. You may be surprised at where they take you.

TIP

It is acceptable and permitted to write an artefact in a foreign language, but the following guidelines must be adhered to:

- The artefact must be written for a specified audience.
- A full translation must be provided and authenticated as being accurate by an expert in translation of the chosen language.
- The accompanying report must be written in English.

ACTIVITY

What links can you find between the different topics in *your* concept map? Try to find at least three possible topics that combine at least two of your ideas.

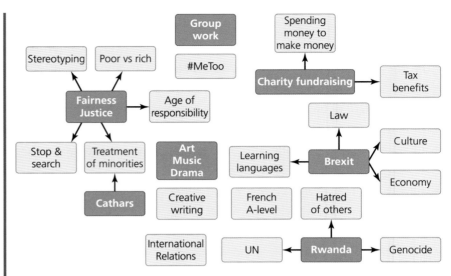

Figure 2.1 Pardeep's concept map showing her ideas

Pardeep finds some interesting links between her initial topic ideas:

- She could produce a piece of creative writing as an artefact, with the plot based on some aspects of Cathar history. This would allow her to undertake primary research in France; she could even write her artefact in French. Her writing could perhaps be a tragic romance, designed for publication in a magazine aimed at French teenagers. Note, however, that Pardeep will receive no particular credit for using French, since she studies it at A-level.
- Pardeep could look at the legal aspects related to some part of Brexit.
- Many Cathars were murdered, as were many Rwandans. Perhaps Pardeep's EP topic could focus in some way on genocide.
- Pardeep could work in a group to raise funds for her work-experience charity.

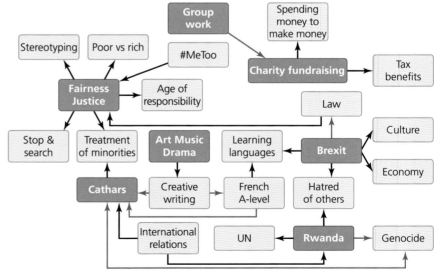

Figure 2.2 Pardeep's concept map with linked ideas

manner of living:
/-ənt/ *adj* ~ing; act
exis·ten·tial·ism /
(deriving from
(1813—55), the D
larized by Sartre /'

 Example

Isla is an EPQ student who is studying French, English Literature and Religious Studies at A-level (with Religious Studies including the study of the Philosophy of Religion). She has decided to undertake an EP that will investigate the philosophical ideas of Albert Camus related to existentialism, as found in his novel *L'Étranger*. This allows Isla to combine skills and interests from all three of her A-levels (without any dual accreditation).

Choosing your EP topic is an exciting process, and once you have decided your topic you will be ready to spend 90 hours studying something that is uniquely 'yours'. But this choice is not easy. The following section provides you with assistance in choosing a topic that will help you meet the criteria of the qualification.

Choosing a suitable topic

When making your choice it might be a good idea to check out the websites of your preferred HE providers, if relevant, as they may offer advice about this. For example, the University of Sheffield stresses that, 'The EPQ should be in a **relevant** subject'. In other words, this university would prefer an EP that is of direct relevance to the undergraduate course being applied for.

To be suitable, an EP topic must satisfy certain criteria:

- You should not already know much about the topic.
- You should not have strong personal opinions or beliefs related to this topic, as these might affect your ability to remain objective.
- The topic should encourage analysis. Simply wanting 'to find out about…' something is not a good topic.
- Ideally there should be a wide range of options, opinions and data related to the topic, to allow you to weigh up the evidence and draw conclusions.
- The topic needs to be of a scope and size that is manageable within 90 hours of independent study at A-level standard. Note that even if your school or college enters you for the EPQ in Year 12, it is still judged at A-level standard.
- Resources related to this topic must be both available to you *and* understandable by you.
- Research into this topic must be ethically acceptable.
- There should be no time restrictions related to this topic that challenge your ability to complete by the submission date.
- The topic must not derive directly from any of your other Level 3 studies. It must genuinely **extend beyond** your main programme of study.
- If the product is an artefact, it must serve some purpose and there needs to be a means of testing its fitness for that purpose.
- You must have a real wish to research this topic; it must come from a **genuine** desire to satisfy your curiosity.

TIP

Do not try to speed up your initial investigation of potential topics. If you choose in haste you may come to regret your choice.

ACTIVITY

Conduct a test for suitability. Go back to your concept map(s) (see page 14) and delete any topics that do not satisfy the bullet points listed here. If you are initially unsure, undertake some preliminary research and be prepared to reject unsuitable ideas. Do *not* stick doggedly to your initial ideas.

Once you have mulled over your ideas, why not share them with a friend, family member or your EPQ group?

It is always helpful to get input from others, but be sure to record any advice or suggestions that you receive — write them in your research journal or blog, if you have chosen to use one. When you feel ready you can share these early ideas with your supervisor. Your supervisor can advise you about any school/ college restrictions on time or resources that might affect your choices.

If you find, based on these suitability criteria, that you have rejected most/ many of your topics then do not worry. You may have to make several attempts before you find some suitable topics.

Working titles

Once you feel comfortable with some potential topics, you can start to formulate possible working titles for each idea/topic. Your supervisor should ask you some searching questions, such as:

- Do the working title of your proposed project and the proposed actions allow you to access the **higher-level concepts and skills** in the qualification — i.e. to plan, research, analyse, evaluate and explain, rather than simply to describe and narrate?
- Are the working title and proposed actions clear and focused on an issue that can be managed by you within the **timescale** and **word total** (5000 words for non-artefact projects), using the available **resources**?
- Do the working title and proposed actions indicate that you will be capable of **independently** investigating and researching the topic?
- Is there a danger that you will be unable to approach the project **impartially** or in a balanced way?
- Are you likely to face difficulties **understanding** the concepts associated with the project topic?

Let us now look carefully at how to avoid the most common errors in choosing a working title.

Analysis

Ensure that your title encourages analysis. Research followed by the re-telling of discovered facts does not encourage analysis. Many titles will require a little 'scene setting' and will inevitably have some descriptive content, but to reach the high-level criteria you need a working title for which there is sufficient research material. You should be able to critically analyse **different** opinions, ideas, techniques, etc. to reach a well-judged conclusion of your own.

 Example

A description of the pharmaceutical properties of the most recent drugs in use for a particular disease or medical condition may well be interesting for you. It will not encourage analysis, however, if all you do is demonstrate that you have understood these properties sufficiently to write about them in your own words.

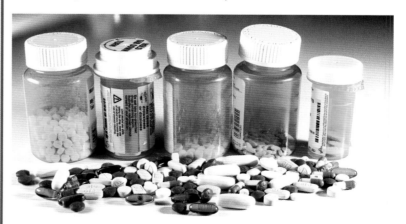

Research

Ensure that your title encourages you to include material, ideas or opinions that you have researched for your EP. If you choose a working title related to a topic with which you are already very familiar, there is a real danger that you will write from your 'own knowledge' rather than from research undertaken specifically for your EP. There needs to be a sense that you are genuinely stepping into unknown territory and **extending** your knowledge and understanding.

 Example

If you have been an avid fan of football all your life, it might not be sensible to compose a football-related working title, unless there are aspects of football about which you know very little and have no particular opinions.

Timescale

Ensure that you have considered the demands of the title with respect to the project timescale. Clearly this partly depends on how the EPQ is delivered in your school or college, but this is not the only factor. Practical collection of data can be very **time-consuming**. Experiments take time to set up, opinions canvassed by post or email can be slow to arrive, artefact testing by an appropriate user needs to be arranged at a time when the user is available, and so on.

Practicalities

Ensure that you have considered the costs and practicalities related to your working title. If you are planning to build or create some form of artefact, think about who will provide/pay for the required **tools and materials**. Make sure that you have the skills required to work with these tools and materials.

TIP

If you are planning research that will require questionnaire responses, do not underestimate how long it takes to create, pilot, improve, distribute, collect and analyse a questionnaire.

🔍 Example

Maybe you would like to record an album of songs as an artefact project, with the songs written by you in a particular designated style. Do you have access to the musical instruments required? Who will the singers be? Do you have access to adequate recording hardware and software? If you get access to these materials, who will teach you to use them? Who will you ask to judge whether the album meets the objectives you have set and comment on the quality of the outcome?

Interviews

Ensure that you have checked your interviewees are **willing** to be interviewed. If you require interview data in order to fully respond to your title, make sure that your proposed interviewees are available for the interviews.

🔍 Example

If you are planning to research some aspect of medicine or dentistry, do not assume that a health professional will have the time to talk to you about your project. Dentists, doctors and nurses are usually very busy and fully employed.

Laboratory research

Ensure that you have checked out the availability of laboratories if you are planning to undertake a **scientific experiment**. You will not be allowed to use laboratories without supervision. Make sure someone (e.g. science teacher or lab technician) has agreed to supervise, but not interfere with, your laboratory research.

Resources

Ensure that you have adequately checked you will be able to access your proposed **research sources**. For any proposed working title, you must have a sound research base, with real, appropriate and reliable resources to form a strong foundation that you can build your Proposal on. Do not just assume that appropriate books and websites can be found. Spend time seeking out good sources and evaluating them to establish the feasibility of your research project. Check that you will be able to access the sources that you need to use. If you are under 18, for example, there are organisations/establishments that will not allow you to visit without an accompanying adult.

Complexity

Ensure that you have fully considered the complexity of your chosen research materials. Do not underestimate how hard certain research materials may be to **understand**. It is better to reject a potential topic at an early stage than to hope that somehow you will come to understand this material later.

Objectivity

Think very carefully before choosing a topic for your EP that is very close to you or that encourages an **emotive response**. It is hard to remain objective about such topics, and your own opinions or beliefs should not become the focus of your EP. This qualification requires objective research, and your conclusions should be based on research evidence, not on your personal opinions. You may feel interested in a subject that is very close to you, for example an illness that has affected a family member or an aspect of politics with a particular family-related historical link but it is hard to remain objective in such situations and your own opinions or beliefs should not become the focus of your EP.

Word total

Ensure that the title can be adequately addressed in 5000 words (this is not relevant for artefact projects, see Chapter 1). You may be attempting to cover too much ground which will inevitably lead to insufficient depth. Conversely, you may have selected a topic that is too limited so that your report is likely to be considerably shorter than 5000 words.

You should discuss your working-title suggestions with your supervisor. Listen carefully to the advice and suggestions that they offer you, but remember that these are suggestions only — you do *not* have to follow them. This is *your* EP; do not let anyone take decisions for you.

Do not worry about the exact wording of your working title. It is the potential and feasibility of your chosen working title that is important at this stage. The precise wording of the title can change once your detailed research has started, following project approval.

19

Aims and objectives

When putting forward your Project Proposal to your supervisor and centre coordinator, you need to give an outline of the initial aims and objectives for your EP.

You need to be clear in your mind about the difference between an aim and an objective:

- A project **aim** is what you want to achieve.
- A project **objective** is how you are going to achieve it.

Your project may have just one **aim**, or it may have two or three aims. In order to achieve your aims, you must set yourself **objectives**. You need to think about the different activities that you will need to engage in to achieve your aims. You will probably need to complete several objectives in order to achieve each aim.

Example

Deepak states: 'The aims of my project are to design and deliver a series of lessons aimed at Year 6 children, giving them an introduction to British Sign Language (BSL).'

Deepak sets himself the following initial objectives:

- I must observe lessons with Year 6 children and read relevant literature so that my lessons are age-appropriate, are of a suitable duration, use appropriate language, etc.
- I must learn BSL myself.
- I must find a group of Year 6 children at a school that will allow me to trial, develop and deliver my lessons.
- I must undertake research into the teaching of BSL to children.
- I must undertake a full risk assessment: do I need a Disclosure and Barring Service (DBS) check? Do I need to obtain parental permission for each child I teach?

When you have formulated a set of working titles that each have clear aims and objectives, ask yourself the following questions.

Are there any working titles related to my EP topics that:

- could be of particular benefit to me in my future career/education?
- look like they will take much longer to complete than the others — do any of these working titles look potentially too big/small for an EP?
- I might not be able to do full justice to because I might struggle to obtain the required resources?
- I am really interested in and genuinely motivated by?

Take your final set of topics, working titles, and aims and objectives to discuss with your supervisor and choose the one that is the best fit for you as an individual.

TIP

Remember to make notes (in your blog or journal if you have started one) about everything related to your EP, including all your rejected ideas, topics and working titles. Eventually you will be writing your Record of Initial Ideas in your Production Log, and one of the things you will be assessed on is your decision making. You should explain in your Production Log **why** any ideas, topics or working titles have been rejected.

TIP

Try to find a variety of different resources, even at this early stage. Do not rely on just one or two. You should set out to investigate your topic from as many different angles as you can.

Group projects

Note that group projects can be very successful, but that each group member must have a clearly defined individual role within the group. The group has **shared aims**, but each member must have **individual and unique objectives** and must work independently on their own individual area of research. The various individual strands of research then come together to realise the product, which will be an artefact of some kind. Each member of the group writes a unique and individual research report, delivers a unique and individual presentation, and completes a unique and individual Production Log. Each group member's input into the group project must represent a minimum of 90 hours of independent work.

 Example

Consider a group that decides to work together to put on a fashion show to raise money for a chosen charity. The members of the group share these aims, but each individual has different objectives related to their individual role within the group:

- One member of the group undertakes research into fundraising for charities, seeking to maximise the funds raised.
- Another member of the group focuses on event management, undertaking research to ensure that all the practicalities of the event are successful.
- A third member of the group focuses on research related to the fashion clothing that will be on display.

Initial resources

Once both you and your supervisor are satisfied that you have found a good working title, with initial aims and objectives that will help you to meet the criteria by which your EP will be judged (see Appendix 5), you must now set about finding a suitable set of initial resources. Chapter 4 focuses on the detailed scrutiny that you should undertake for each source used for your project. Even at this pre-approval stage you must convince your supervisor that you have a valid and reliable starting place from which appropriate research can be undertaken.

 Example

Joe's intended product is an artefact, a recipe book containing local recipes from his home county. He established through his research that there are no such books available. As initial resources, Joe has found ten other regional recipe books so that he can fully analyse their characteristics. Joe has emailed several publishers of recipe books and an editor has agreed to a telephone interview. In order to finance the publication of his book Joe has started to think about his budget. He has details of three different self-publication firms. Joe has emailed all the Women's Institute (WI) groups in his county and has already received several recipes from WI members. Joe has a team of willing testers to try and taste the recipes for him. He has visited the local library and found two books written by authors with excellent credentials, which have sections in them with references to the culinary specialities of his county.

Joe is confident that his successful research so far means that, if his centre coordinator approves his Proposal, he will be able to add to his resources and create a recipe book that is firmly based on sound research.

Once you have a good research base that both your supervisor and you are happy with, it is time to start writing your **Production Log**. The **Record of Initial Ideas** (page 5 of the AQA Production Log) should record all the different ideas that you explored, expanded and rejected, as well as the idea that you intend to put forward as a formal Proposal. You can include here details about the ways in which you have satisfied yourself that your chosen initial sources will be suitable (or you may prefer to record this information elsewhere, perhaps using some form of source evaluation table; the choice is entirely yours). Use your blog or journal to remind yourself of the various decisions made at the beginning of your research journey. Explain **why** you rejected some ideas. On this page of your Production Log you have the opportunity to explain why your final topic choice is of interest to you.

The Project Proposal

The Project Proposal comes in three parts (pages 6–8 of the AQA Production Log).

You complete **Proposal Part A**, your supervisor completes **Proposal Part B** and your centre coordinator completes **Proposal Part C**.

1 You declare in Part A that the Proposal is your own choice and work, following negotiation with your supervisor.

   When filling in Part A you should give as much detail as you can. You are trying to convince your centre coordinator that you have a very well-considered Proposal for your project.

   • **Do not** worry about the precise wording of your working title. Even at this stage, however, the title should enable you to draw an evidence-based conclusion, with the evidence coming from your proposed research.

   • **Do** give as much detail as you can about the initial resources that you have found. There is no need to repeat information about the scrutiny of these sources, however, if you have included it in the Record of Initial Ideas.

   • **Do** explain how this particular topic has ignited your curiosity and interest.

   • **Do** clearly state what your intended product is at the time of proposal. This does *not* mean that you have to stick rigidly to your proposed outcome. If your research leads you in a direction which means your final product is different to that proposed at this stage, this will be perfectly acceptable provided you demonstrate clearly that the change has been driven by research. This is discussed in further detail in Chapter 5.

   • **Do not** forget to clearly state the courses of study that you are following alongside the EPQ. This is important. You need to demonstrate that you are not falling foul of 'dual accreditation' and that you are not duplicating work that will be credited for other qualifications.

   Note that at the Proposal stage you are clearly warned about unfair practice, including plagiarism. This is covered in Chapter 5. Remember that there is only one person you will be cheating if you submit work that is not wholly your own, and that is *you*.

2 Your supervisor declares in Part B that your Proposal is feasible and appropriate as a project *and* that there is no likely dual accreditation of assessed project work (i.e. no significant overlap with work related to your other Level 3 courses).

3 Your centre coordinator declares in Part C that they have:
   • approved your Proposal
   • approved your Proposal subject to written recommendations
   • not approved your Proposal.

   In the unlikely event that your Project Proposal is rejected, you must carefully read the reasons for rejection, discuss them with your supervisor, then go right back to the beginning of the process and try to find a more suitable topic, working title, and aims and objectives.

   In the event that your Proposal has been approved subject to certain written recommendations, these recommendations *must* be followed. Usually they will require you to develop or change something related to your aims or your objectives.

ACTIVITY

Complete the tick list below to judge whether you are ready to submit your Proposal.

Topic choice:

- Am I fully committed to my chosen topic? ☐

- Will I be able to maintain interest and passion for this topic? ☐

Working title:

- Will this title help me fulfil the demands of the specification criteria? ☐

- Have I carefully considered the risks associated with this title? ☐

- Am I confident that I have a sound research base relevant to this title? ☐

Aims and objectives:

- Am I clear about what I am hoping to achieve? ☐

- Have I identified objectives that will enable me to achieve my aims? ☐

Artefact (if appropriate):

- Does my intended artefact have a clear purpose? ☐

- Does my intended artefact have a well-defined audience/user? ☐

- Am I clear in my mind about how my artefact might be tested for its fitness for purpose? ☐

Group (if appropriate):

- Has the group carefully considered the group aim? ☐

- Do I have clear individual objectives? ☐

- Do I fully understand how my individual research links to that undertaken by other members of the group? ☐

Time management:

- Have I created a broad plan, including a set of objectives that will enable me to achieve my aims? ☐

- Have I estimated how long it will take me to achieve each objective? ☐

- Have I identified time in my week that can be used for the EPQ? ☐

CHECKLIST

Do I understand:

☐ why some topics might not be suitable for an EP?

☐ the difference between an aim and an objective?

☐ the importance of an initial resource base?

☐ what is required of me when I write my project proposal?

☐ that using a personal journal or blog will help me keep notes that can be used when I complete pages in my Log?

3

The Project Plan

Once you have received approval from your coordinator you should prepare for your **Planning Review** meeting with your supervisor. At this meeting, you will put forward your Project Plan to your supervisor.

A detailed Project Plan is *not* a plan for your report. It is a plan that takes into account your use of time and resources as you set yourself clear, achievable objectives.

When completing the Planning Review page of your Log you *must* address any recommendations made by your coordinator. If approval is dependent on these recommendations then you must clearly show that you understand what is required of you. For example, your coordinator may require you to carry out a full risk assessment to demonstrate that you are fully aware of the risks associated with your proposal and have put appropriate control measures in place (see Appendix 1). Alternatively, your coordinator may require you to carry out an assessment related to the ethics of your proposed research, to ensure that all appropriate considerations are in place (see Appendix 2).

When considering your plan, you should consider the types of resource you might need to use, the time available to you and how best this can be used.

Time management

Good time management is the key to success in the EPQ. In order to achieve this, you must plan carefully and then protect your plan. There will be many competing demands on your time and ultimately *you* are the one who decides how your time will most effectively be used. There is no particular time management approach that you must follow and there is no specific template that you must use. You will not be told by your supervisor exactly how to manage your time — it will be up to you.

ACTIVITY

Every day you spend 24 hours doing something. How do you spend your time?

Starting from this present moment, work back through the last 24 hours and itemise exactly what you have done:

- How many hours were you asleep?
- How many hours/minutes were spent cooking/eating meals?
- How many hours/minutes were spent dressing/washing, etc.?
- How many hours were spent exercising/playing sport?
- How many hours were spent in lessons/lectures?
- How many hours were spent working on homework?
- How many hours were spent undertaking paid/voluntary work?

- How many hours were spent watching/interacting with a screen? (TV/laptop/phone/tablet)
- How many hours were spent travelling?

Does your list add up to 24 hours?

What else did you spend time doing? Try to fill in the missing hours.

Having looked at a single day, expand the exercise to contain a whole week. Are you surprised at how your time slips away? Were there any activities that are less important than others? Were there any activities that took up more of your time than perhaps they should? Are there some activities that you *have* to do (sleeping and eating, for example)? Are some parts of your day more productive than others (are you an early-bird or a night-owl?)? Most importantly: will you be able to find the time to fit in independent study focused on your EP?

TIP

The most common admission from EPQ students when reflecting on the success, or otherwise, of their project is that their planning was not strong. In particular they admit to **poor time management** and that they underestimated how long certain tasks would take them.

Rest and relaxation are important for your physical and mental well-being, and good time management does *not* require that every hour of every day is spent working. What is required is an awareness that you have control over how you spend/manage your time.

Students' Logs frequently record issues that have caused them problems with their time management. Procrastination comes high on the list and students often report that they find myriad 'reasons' preventing them from tackling the objective at hand. In particular, the use of social media and mobile phones causes interruptions to study.

How much time do you spend on your mobile phone each day?

TIP

Do not rush to book your Planning Review meeting with your supervisor. Careful planning takes time — do not go to your Planning meeting until you have created a detailed plan.

Many students report that lack of self-discipline resulted in their failure to protect the time they had allocated to their EP work. Crucially, however, students report that they had underestimated how big the tasks were that they had set themselves, both in terms of availability of information and, more frequently, in terms of how long the tasks would take to complete.

Unexpected and unplanned-for events or illness cause problems for students when no 'slack' time has been built into their planning. An important part of your planning is to build in time to deal with the unexpected. Do not plan to use every single hour of your allocated time for an intended purpose. It is vital that some slack time is included in your plan so that when you run into a problem you have capacity to adjust your plan and achieve your objectives. Good planners build in safety margins and are ready to deal with adverse circumstances, should these arise.

ACTIVITY

Here is an exercise you can do either alone or with a friend. Come up with a short list of tasks and then estimate how long it will take you to complete each task. Now complete each task and see how good your estimates were.

Example tasks:

- Find and write down the titles of ten novels by Stephen King.
- Translate your favourite nursery rhyme into a language you studied up to GCSE.

- Find the names and constituencies of five female Members of Parliament, each representing a different political party.
- Create a PowerPoint presentation with five slides that explains your EP proposal to a Year 11 class (this could be saved as a useful starting point for your EP presentation).

How good were your estimates? If you, like most people, underestimated how long it actually takes to complete even simple tasks, use this knowledge to make sensible estimates about the time required to complete tasks related to your EP.

SMART objectives

Your project will have one or more aims. For example:

- You are seeking an answer to a specific research question.
- You intend to write a film script/short story/magazine article.
- You intend to test a stated hypothesis.
- You aim (as a member of a group putting on a performance) to create a full set of costumes.

In order to achieve your aim, you need **objectives**. Objectives are the actions/tasks planned and undertaken by you to enable you to achieve your aim. Your Project Plan should clearly set out your objectives, and at this stage you need to consider these in greater depth. It is a good idea to make sure that your objectives are 'SMART'. The acronym SMART sometimes has different words used for some of the letters, but a generally accepted set of words is given here.

SMART objectives are:

- Specific
- Measurable
- Achievable
- Relevant
- Time-related

Example

Martyn is setting himself objectives for his EP on virus transmission.

To have an objective such as 'I will go to the library and read some books about viruses' is **not SMART**.

The objective 'I will go to the city library on Saturday morning and stay for two hours. I will find at least one book that has relevant sections related to virus transmission between human beings and take at least one side of A4 notes' is more focused.

- It is **Specific** — Martyn knows exactly what he will be doing (looking at virus transmission).
- It is **Measurable** — Martyn will take at least one side of notes.
- It is **Achievable** — it is reasonable to think that Martyn can write one side of notes in two hours and also reasonable to think Martyn can find a book with the required information at the library.
- It is **Relevant** — this activity will clearly help Martyn research his EPQ.
- Finally, it is **Time-related**, in that it will take Martyn two hours to complete. Understanding the time that it takes to complete his objectives will help him with his planning.

Martyn may not achieve his objective, but because it is **SMART** it will be clear to him if he has not achieved it. He will be able to adjust his project planning to take account of this.

Reasons for not achieving his objective may include:

- On Saturday Martyn's younger sister was taken ill and Martyn was required to stay at home to care for her.
- The library had a fire drill and Martyn's visit was cut short to 90 minutes.
- Martyn's book-searching took up most of his allotted time, but he found other relevant and useful books relating to other aspects of his EP.
- Martyn took no notes at the library but was allowed to borrow the book and will be able to take notes on Sunday evening.
- Martyn spent too much time playing computer games at home and was very late getting to the library.

An important aspect of planning involves forward thinking. How can you succeed in achieving your aims even if certain objectives are not met? It is a good idea to have an alternative set of objectives that can be brought into your plan, should the need arise.

TIP
Failing to achieve a SMART objective is not a crime, but using objectives that have real clarity allows you to judge whether or not your project planning is on track.

ACTIVITY

For your chosen working title, set out at least three objectives and clearly demonstrate how each one is SMART using a table like this:

Table 3.1 Set SMART objectives: Specific, Measurable, Achievable, Relevant, Time-related

Working title:			
	Objective	Objective	Objective
Specific: State precisely what it is that you intend to do			
Measurable: Give quantifiable parameters to your objective, so that you can judge exactly when it has been achieved			
Achievable: Check that you are able to achieve this objective — do you have all the required skills, resources and permissions?			
Relevant: Keeping your EP aims in mind, how will this objective help you achieve your aim?			
Time-related: Does this objective have a clear starting time? Have you estimated how long it will take to achieve it?			

What type of planning works for you?

There is no prescribed planning method that you must follow for your EP, but learning to use some form of effective planning will be a valuable skill for use in your later life.

When considering your Project Plan it may well help to create an ideas diagram. You might consider creating an online whiteboard with http://sketchboard.io or you might start with a large blank piece of paper and a pencil. Your ideas diagram should include all the different factors you can think of that relate to your project. This will help you see that completion of a project of this scale will need careful management and that this is entirely down to your planning and organisation.

Ben had his EP proposal approved in April. Ben is an avid fan of *Game of Thrones* and he heard that the Scythians may have been used by George R.R. Martin as an inspiration when he created the Dothraki characters in his books. Ben would like to study Archaeology at university. His EP has been narrowed down to a focused investigation into aspects of Scythian culture, but until he researches further he is not sure where his final focus will be. He intends to go to the exhibition on the Scythians at the British Museum, which is on from the following September through to January.

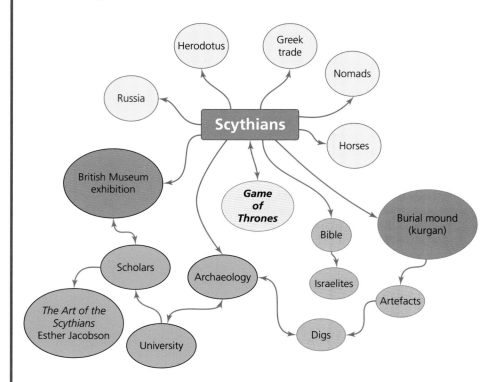

Figure 3.1 Ben's concept map showing his ideas

Initial background reading to learn more about Ben's chosen topic can be done in any small time slots that he identifies. For example, when travelling by train to college or during study periods at school. Visiting the exhibition related to Ben's topic at the British Museum, however, will need more careful planning, including thinking about transport to get there. Will he make this trip at a weekend or during a vacation? Will he travel alone or try to find a companion?

As well as identifying objectives that are essential in order to achieve your aim, you should also identify in your week/term/year slots of time that you can allocate to your EP. Every project is unique but here are some examples of areas that you might need to consider in your project planning:

- Are there any periods of the year when I will *not* be able to undertake certain aspects of my project? (For example, have you factored in the demands that will be made on your time when you come to complete your UCAS form?)
- Am I intending to undertake some form of primary research?

- Are there certain people who I need to interview?
- How long should each stage of my project take?
- Are there any restrictions on my access to materials, equipment, places, etc.?
- Are some aspects of my research dependent on other aspects? Will my research activities need to be structured?
- How long should I allow for my artefact to be tested (if relevant)?
- Are there any risks that I will need to consider and do I need to put any control measures in place?

ACTIVITY

For your approved EP proposal:

- Create an ideas diagram, including all the factors that you can think of related to your project.

- Identify tasks that need to be done in order to complete your EP. Some of these tasks can be done in small time slots, others will need larger time slots.

- Try to match up the time you have available with the identified tasks.

Remember to include:

- How you intend to 'test' your artefact (if appropriate).

- How your individual research journeys will combine to create the product that you are working on as a group (if appropriate).

There are various things that you need to think about when developing your plan. For example, do you work best:

- at home
- at school or college
- at the city/university library
- in your local coffee shop?

How will you take notes, collect data and organise your research? Will you:

- set up a Pinterest page of relevant images
- use an online whiteboard
- store files on your laptop (how often will you back this up?)
- use pen-and-ink hard-copy notes in a notebook
- use an EPQ folder provided for you on your school's or college's IT system?

It is not unusual to read in an EPQ Log that a student has lost all his/her EPQ work, that their memory stick has corrupted or been lost, or their laptop has been stolen. Good planning includes preparing for such eventualities, for example by using cloud-based storage for your work or using a back-up memory stick. In most cases such eventualities are preventable.

Deadlines

It is a good idea to set yourself deadlines. You may not have done this before, but you are bound to have had deadlines set *for* you. From an early age, you will have been set homework at school and you will have been given a date by which it must be completed. What have been the consequences if you have not completed the homework?

- You received a detention after school.
- You received a low or zero grade.
- You received some other form of sanction.

None of these things will happen if you fail to meet your *own* deadlines.
A key aspect of this qualification is that you are making all your own
decisions. If you choose to let other uses of your time crowd out the time
allocated for your EP, the only thing to suffer will be your EP. If you know
that you have a tendency to be easily distracted, you must develop strategies
to prevent this. Use a planner, diary or calendar and give each SMART
objective a deadline date.

While monitoring your planning, you need to judge each objective in
terms of its **urgency** and its **importance**. As a deadline approaches, the
completion of an objective becomes more urgent — but was the deadline
set for convenience or is the date that was set of real importance?

 Example

Felix is working on a project related to the use of greenfield sites for
building houses in the Selby area. One of his objectives is to complete
the reading of the 'Five-year Housing Land Supply Report for Selby
District Council' by 18 November so that he can be prepared for an
interview with a local planning officer on 21 November.

Imagine that today is 11 November and Felix has not yet completed
this reading. Should he prioritise this reading or change his deadline?

If Felix has not completed the reading by 18 November, he will not
have time to plan for the interview and it will be a wasted opportunity.
Felix should therefore deem this objective to be urgent even though
other aspects of his research are also of great importance.

Felix will therefore prioritise this reading.

Felix has also planned to collect data from residents in the Selby area
by using a questionnaire. He has set himself the deadline to complete
the collection of this primary data by 6 February.

Imagine that today is 3 February and Felix has not completed this data
collection. Should Felix prioritise this data collection or should he
change his deadline?

When Felix reviews his planning, he finds that nothing immediately
depends on the primary data collection. In terms of importance to his
project, the careful analysis of his secondary research is of greater
importance than the primary data collection.

Felix will therefore set a later date as the deadline for the data
collection objective and continue to prioritise his scrutiny of
secondary research data.

Critical paths

When considering deadlines, it is useful to consider whether there are any
critical paths that your objectives should follow. You do not want to find
there are several tasks that cannot be undertaken because they all require
completion of another task, one that you failed to start early enough.
Considering critical paths is a useful way to approach project management.
For each task that you have identified, decide if it is critical or non-critical.
A critical task has other tasks dependent upon its completion. For example,

when building a house, the task of laying the foundations is critical. It would be impossible, moreover, to put the tiles on the roof if the walls have not yet been built, thus building the walls is also a critical task. Laying the tiles on the roof depends first on having the foundations laid and then on having the walls built. Laying the tiles themselves is non-critical, because nothing depends on this task.

ACTIVITY

Harriet has decided to create a working model canal lock to be used as a teaching aid by teachers of Year 5 children.

She identifies several objectives, such as:

- Visit my local canal to observe the lock mechanism.
- Set myself a budget for the model.
- Investigate materials to use in constructing my model.
- Visit the library or search online to find books/ articles describing canal lock mechanisms.
- Interview a teacher of Year 5 to establish optimum size of model and generally discuss the project requirements.
- Visit the local science museum, which has several working models.

- Design my model.
- Test my model with water to check it is watertight.
- Seek permission and clearance to use my model with a class of Year 5 children.
- Set criteria by which I can judge if my model is fit for purpose.
- Paint my model.
- Make or buy items for the canal landscape — trees, boats, animals, etc.

Work through this list of objectives and decide which are critical.

- Can some be undertaken at any time?
- Should some be ordered differently?
- Do some depend on others having been completed?
- What other objectives might she require in order to achieve her aim?

You may have come across the use of critical path analysis for project management. It is not a requirement of your EP planning that you should be able mathematically to calculate and identify a critical path, but it will certainly aid your planning if you can identify those tasks that should be prioritised so that other aspects of your project development are not held up.

Gantt charts

For some students, the Gantt chart offers an easy-to-use visual planning tool. Below is a very simple example of a Gantt chart in Microsoft Excel, created by a student undertaking the EPQ while at college. The college offers the EPQ over a one-year period, starting and finishing in January, aiming for entry in May. The student has timetabled time with her supervisor from mid-January in Year 12 until mid-January in Year 13.

The college has set various deadlines, for example:

- Initial planning must be completed by 10 May in Year 12.
- Project Proposals must be completed by the centre coordinator by 24 May in Year 12.
- Mid-project Reviews must take place by 13 September in Year 13.
- Project Product Reviews must take place by 15 November in Year 13.
- Presentations must take place by 10 January in Year 13.
- Completion of Log books and final hand-in must take place by 24 January in Year 13.

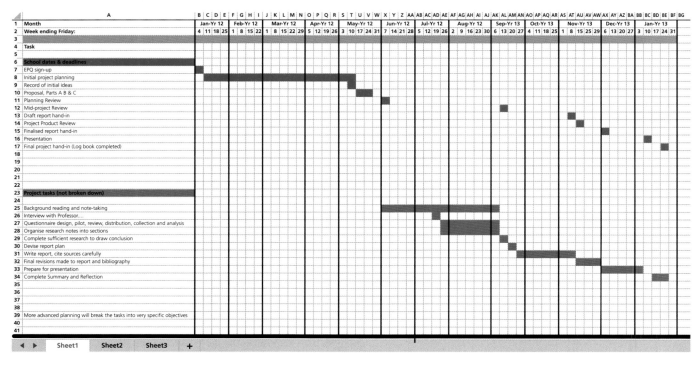

Figure 3.2 A simple example of a Gantt chart in Microsoft Excel

ACTIVITY

For each objective identified by you for *your* EP, try to break it down into smaller objectives. Then for each small objective:

- Estimate how long it will take you to complete.
- Identify any objectives that cannot be achieved until others have been achieved.

In the chart the student has planned how her time will be used in a very broad way. This is acceptable as a first stage of rough planning.

To achieve greater detail, she needs to create a new Gantt chart that breaks her tasks down further into smaller objectives. She may even split the time up into days rather than weeks.

For example, she might include small objectives (not given in any particular order):

- Proofread my report looking for typos that the computer spell-check would not pick up.
- Check every date and quantity derived from a secondary source with a different source, and delete any facts or figures that cannot be independently verified.
- Enrol on and complete an online course to help me understand more about good questionnaire design.
- Produce a summary of my findings so far.

Every student has a unique project and thus every plan will be unique. The following are objectives that might be relevant for three very different projects:

- Ms Cohen to assess my artefact (as an expert in the field).
- Trial my mathematical model and compare the model outputs with the measured outputs achieved in my experiment.
- Spend an afternoon at the Yorkshire Sculpture Park taking notes and photographs. Make sketches of four of the Henry Moore sculptures.

One of the benefits of using a Gantt chart is that it forces you to consider whether one objective is dependent on any others:

- I have to complete the construction of my artefact *before* it is assessed by Ms Cohen.
- I have to create my mathematical model *before* I can test it.
- To get the most benefit from my trip to the Yorkshire Sculpture Park it needs to come *after* my interview with a lecturer at my local art college.

One important thing to understand about using a Gantt chart is that it can be changed as often as you like. For example:

- Some estimated times might prove to be wrong.
- You might realise that there are some key objectives missing.
- You may become aware that a particular activity cannot start until another one has finished.

Action plans

Many students create some form of action plan. This plan might be written in the form of a 'to do' list or it might be created in Excel. The example given below is tabular. An action plan is exactly what it sounds like: a list of actions and planned dates by which the action should be completed. A very simple action plan will contain all your objectives and you can tick them off, one by one, as they are achieved. If you fail to meet a particular planned date you will need to review your action plan, possibly altering several dates in response to the delay that has occurred. This does *not* suggest that your planning was bad. What matters is that you can **explain why** the objective was not achieved as originally planned and that you can **amend** your plan to ensure that your final completion remains on target.

The action plan in Table 3.2 was created by a student at a school that enrols students in September of Year 12 and enters them for the EPQ in November of Year 13. The purple notes give deadlines set by the school for certain parts of the process. The student can put in his own deadlines related to the objectives identified as required for his project. In the right-hand column, the student can record when each objective is *actually* achieved.

Table 3.2 An action plan

Date planned	Objective	Date achieved
28 Sep	EPQ sign-up	
5 Oct	Initial project planning commences First EPQ session with supervisor	
12 Oct		
19 Oct		
26 Oct	Half-term week	
2 Nov	Initial planning complete Submission of Proposal Part A to supervisor	
9 Nov		
16 Nov	Project approval complete	
23 Nov	Planning Review meeting	
30 Nov		
7 Dec		
14 Dec		
21 Dec	Christmas holidays	
28 Dec	Christmas holidays	
4 Jan		
11 Jan		
18 Jan		
25 Jan		
1 Feb		
8 Feb	Mid-project Review	
15 Feb	Half-term week	
22 Feb		
1 Mar		
8 Mar		
15 Mar		
22 Mar		
29 Mar	Easter holidays	
5 Apr	Easter holidays	
12 Apr	Hand in draft report	
19 Apr		
26 Apr	Project Product Review meeting	
3 May		
10 May		
17 May		
24 May	Hand in completed product (report plus artefact)	
31 May	Half-term week	
7 Jun		
14 Jun		
21 Jun		
28 Jun	Presentation week	
5 Jul		
12 Jul	Final deadline for all projects	
19 Jul		

This student is creating an artefact. His working title is 'To research (historically), plan and produce (own needlework) an eighteenth-century ball-gown'. He has decided that a substantial amount of time will be dedicated to his EP during the Easter holiday period. In Table 3.3 he therefore expands the action plan for the fortnight of the Easter holiday.

Table 3.3 An expanded action plan

Mar/Apr (Easter holidays)	Objective
29th	Test artefact: Take my ballgown to local museum for evaluation
30th	Write up notes from interview with museum curator
31st	Photo shoot in local National Trust property, with Gemma as my model
1st	Complete my sketchbook, ensuring all yarn and material samples are firmly attached
2nd	Day off (Good Friday)
3rd	Day off (Easter Saturday)
4th	Day off (Easter Sunday)
5th	Print out relevant photographs showing artefact design and realisation
6th	Integrate the product evaluation from the museum curator into report
7th	Complete my report
8th	Proofread my report
9th	Check all citations
10th	Day off from EP (weekend): Other homework
11th	Day off from EP (weekend): Other homework

ACTIVITY

Using Excel (or another program of your choosing, or a piece of lined paper and a pencil so that you can make alterations easily), create an action plan for your project:

- Include any college/school deadlines.
- Include all the objectives you have already identified.
- Identify which objectives must be ordered, so you know which objectives must be achieved before others can be initiated.
- Decide if, during half-terms and holidays, you intend to have daily targets rather than weekly targets.

TIP

If you need to amend your action plan, change dates, add or change objectives, it would be a good idea to include an annotated set of the evolving action plans in an appendix within your project submission. This will contribute to your evidence of planning and monitoring.

If you decide to use one, be ready to alter your Gantt chart and/or action plan whenever required. Review it frequently so that you can monitor the progress of your Project Plan. As your plan develops you can subdivide objectives and add more detail. One thing to be very clear about in your mind as you put together your EP planning is that you are not expected to be able to see into the future and your planning does not have to be perfect. There may be many changes and additions that you will have to make to your plan once you set off on your project journey. There is nothing wrong with this at all. Your research may take you up an unexpected avenue and this may lead to new or changed aims and/or objectives. You will be expected to monitor the progress of your Project Plan, making amendments whenever necessary and carefully explaining **why** these amendments have come about.

Example

Kosmo has his Project Proposal approved in December and he decides to use an action plan with specified dates to set out his objectives. He chooses to review his plan at the end of each month and amend it as necessary.

When Kosmo created his action plan in December, he planned to spend 15 April, the Easter bank holiday, in the city library, because he knew that he would not be at school that day. But he failed to check whether the library would be open on 15 April. The library turned out to be closed for the bank holiday so Kosmo had to amend his plan.

Kosmo should ask himself questions, for example: *Is there anything else that I can usefully do on 15 April that does not depend on the library research having been completed? Can I find another day when I will be able to go to the library instead?*

Kosmo should amend his action plan, making sure that any critical paths have not been upset.

Remember, there is no prescribed or essential method of planning that you must use for your EP. If your school or college gives you a template to use, it is perfectly acceptable to politely refuse it and use whatever form of planning works best for you. Indeed, this is one way in which you can take control of your EP. If you *have* used any software, diagrams or tools to help you plan your EP, you should refer to them when you write up the Planning Review page of your Log.

TIP

Do not forget to include in your EP Planning Review how you intend to monitor your project progress.

TIP

Some students find EP planning works best for them using a large year-to-view wall calendar with coloured mini sticky notes/ stickers that can be moved around.

CHECKLIST

Do I understand:

☐ what project planning should include?

☐ that I must protect the time I have allocated to my EP?

☐ that I will need to be self-disciplined in my approach to my EP?

☐ that there is a range of planning tools and that I can choose the one that best suits me?

4 Resources

What counts as a resource?

When thinking about research for your EP, you may think that your research will involve using 'books and the internet', a phrase commonly seen in EPQ Production Logs. There is a wealth of other potential research resources, however, and a successful EP will contain research from a wide variety of **relevant** resources. Depending on the nature of your EP, you may have a very different set of resources to other students as they undertake their own, different EP. Let us consider for a moment what might count as an EP resource.

A student creating some form of artefact might include online tutorials or training manuals as part of their research. They may, for example, need to learn new practical skills. In some instances, they may even need to enrol on a short training course. Artefact projects will frequently involve the use of tools, software, materials, etc. All of these are appropriate resources.

 Example

For her EP, Lucy has decided to design and create a wedding dress for her cousin, working with a fixed budget. One aspect of research that Lucy should undertake relates to the use of appropriate tools and materials.

Lucy intends to interview her cousin to get very clear ideas about her preferences. Following this interview Lucy will:

- obtain swatches of the fabrics she has selected as possible materials from which to make the dress
- try out sewing these fabrics using different sewing machines and techniques so that she can select the best machine and most appropriate stitching

- experiment with different gauge sewing-machine needles, different strengths and types of sewing-thread, different stitch lengths, etc.
- look at online forums that discuss techniques for successfully stitching fine fabrics, such as silk and satin

All of these activities form part of her research.

For an artefact project, any decision made by an EPQ student that relates to techniques or materials used in the making of the artefact should be firmly based on evidence gathered by research. This research can take many different forms.

For some students, the expert opinion of certain academics or skilled practitioners may be of huge value to their research. For these students, a valuable resource could be an e-mail interchange or an interview transcript, if they are lucky enough to make personal contact with experts in their chosen field of research. If personal communication is not possible then it may be possible to find a recorded interview from which the expert's opinions can be ascertained.

 ## Example

Gaya is undertaking an EP related to the health of teeth in dogs. She has arranged to do a one-week work placement at her local veterinary practice. While there, she hopes to conduct some brief interviews with the various employees at the practice, asking very specific questions about any first-hand experiences the employees have had relating to the health of dogs' teeth. This interview data could be useful for her EP.

There is a wide variety of research resources that might help with your EP. Blogs, published government reports, films, podcasts, television and radio programmes, Hansard transcripts, photographs and physical data gathered on a field trip are all potential EP resources. Books and scholarly articles published either online or in academic journals can also be valuable sources of information. Indeed, anything from which you can extract reliable and relevant information or data that relates to your project topic can be counted as a resource. The key thing to remember when undertaking an EP is that your research should be **relevant** and **in-depth**, and that you should seek out a **wide** a range of resources.

See Appendix 4 for more potential resources that you might consider for your EP.

See Appendix 4 for more potential resources that you might consider for your EP.

ACTIVITY

For your chosen EP topic, see if you can find at least one resource of each of the following types:

- A magazine article.
- A newspaper article.
- A peer-reviewed article from an academic journal.

- A book.
- The name of a potential interviewee.
- Some form of experiment or survey you could use to gather data.
- Somewhere to visit that will offer relevant information or data.

TIP

Keep careful records of *every* resource that you consider for your EP, even the ones that you later decide not to use. It is important that you communicate how you have selected the resources that you eventually do make use of.

Note that it is *not* appropriate for most students doing the EPQ to conduct a survey or experiment. But for some students their choice of EP topic has been driven by a wish to develop skills in data collection and analysis. It *would* be appropriate for these students to include some form of experiment or survey in their research.

What is important at this early stage of your project is for you to explore as many possible avenues of research as you can. Later in this chapter we will discuss how you can decide which of the resources you have found should be used as part of your EP research. Do not rush into avenues of research without fully considering the options available.

Don't worry if you can't initially find many different types of resource for your EP, but be ready to explain why this is not possible in your Log.

Primary and secondary sources

Generally speaking, sources of information can be divided into two types, primary and secondary. There is no requirement for you to use both of these types of resource. As you embark on your EP, one of the first tasks is to consider what types of data and resources might be required to meet your objectives.

Primary sources involve some form of direct collection of data. **Secondary** sources are produced by scholars/journalists/authors referring to an event or data collection after the event or data collection has happened.

Primary sources

Primary sources may be found in museum archives and may include objects that have survived from the past, such as photographs, maps or articles of clothing. Original literary works or original works of art are also considered to be primary sources. Letters, e-mails, eyewitness accounts and original official records are all primary sources.

Any information that you collect from primary sources is called **primary data**. Visits to museums or art galleries to collect primary data may be useful for certain EPs, as you can experience the relevant resources first-hand.

41

Interviews, surveys, experiments and questionnaires are also primary sources. The data that you gather through field studies, direct observation, experiments, surveys, questionnaires and interviews is primary data.

If you collect and use primary data in your EP you are doing **primary research**.

Example

Rio undertook an EP on stress experienced by primates living in zoos. As part of his research he spent four days at his local zoo, patiently observing and recording the frequency of certain behaviours displayed by selected primates. These direct observations provided primary data that Rio went on to analyse in the context of the information he had gathered from books and articles.

This data collection was very time-consuming, but Rio valued the opportunity to observe first-hand the stress-related behaviours that he had read about in various written resources.

Primary data gathered from experiments, observations or surveys is called **raw data**. You can use this data to conduct statistical analysis. Statistical methods for the analysis of data can be found in Appendix 3.

Quantitative and qualitative data

Primary data can be either quantitative or qualitative.

Quantitative data is information that is measurable with numbers, for example the answers to questions such as: How many cows in this field have white on their face? How tall are you? How many siblings do you have?

The resulting data will involve a numerical measure, for example 80% of cows, 150 cm, three brothers and one sister.

Qualitative data involves information that is not measurable, including information about people's beliefs and opinions. For example, the answers to questions such as: What do you feel about Sunday trading laws? In what circumstances, if any, would you approve of the reintroduction of the death penalty?

Answers are likely to be descriptive, such as:

> I have mixed feelings about Sunday trading. On the one hand I find it very convenient to know that if I run out of milk the supermarket will be open for most of the day, but on the other hand I understand that some employees will be given no choice about working on a Sunday.

Appendix 3 offers advice relating to the analysis of both quantitative and qualitative data.

Primary research for artefacts

EPQ students creating artefacts frequently include some form of direct data gathering; this is **primary research**.

Example

Alex decided to create some works of art based on the growth of mould on fruit. He researched how long it would take for the mould to reach the growth that he required for his artworks. (He took care with respect to health and safety and did a full risk assessment.) Alex planned his project carefully — he undertook trials to find the best procedures to follow in order to grow 'beautiful' mould. Alex carefully recorded everything he did and all the decisions taken, so that the reader of his project would understand how this primary research contributed to his final product.

> **TIP**
>
> If you are planning to grow or breed a living organism, be aware of the time available to you.

How to use people as part of your research

People can be used as part of your research in a variety of ways. You could conduct some form of experiment involving human research participants, to collect primary research data. You could collect responses to questionnaires or include interview responses as part of your research. You could use focus groups, particularly where an artefact has been designed for a particular audience. Note, however, that there is no specification requirement that you must use people as part of your research.

Scrutiny of *all* potential resources is important, including any proposed primary research that involves collection of data directly from human research participants. People may lie, exaggerate or omit key pieces of evidence. Everyone will have personal opinions and beliefs that may affect the way they respond to questions or view events.

Any use of people within your research should be subject to careful consideration of the ethics related to research (see Appendix 2). In all cases you should use the data in a confidential way (e.g. not using participants' names in your EP report unless they give permission) and assure your participants of this. All research participants should also be asked to give informed consent that data collected from them may be used as part of your EP. Research participants must always have the right to withdraw from the research activity at any point.

If you intend to write to specific people to invite them to help you with your research, take care to write a carefully worded, grammatically correct and polite letter or e-mail, such as the example on page 44. Use a formal mode of address and explain in your letter or e-mail when and where you have come across them as a potential resource for your EP. Be clear on what you are asking them to do and how the data will be used.

> EPQ Academy
> The High Street
> Anytown
> XX2 3YY
>
> 23 October
>
> Dear Doctor Gamlen,
>
> I am a student at EPQ Academy in Anytown, currently completing my A-level studies in Year 13. Alongside my A-levels I am undertaking the Extended Project Qualification. For my project, I am investigating costs relating to the development and production of new drugs by small pharmaceutical companies. (I am hoping to study Pharmacy next year at university.) While researching I have discovered that Gamlen Instruments produce tablet-making machines. From your website I have learned that 'The Gamlen M Series offers a quick route to the manufacture of small batches of tablets under tightly controlled conditions'. I am very keen to learn more about the small-scale manufacture of tablets and I am writing to ask you if you would be prepared to answer a few questions to help me with my research project. While your insights would be very helpful for my research, I will not quote you directly in the research report unless you are happy for me to do so.
> If you are willing to be questioned I could send you the questions via email for you to answer at some time that is convenient to you. Alternatively, we could perhaps arrange a ten-minute telephone or Skype interview.
>
> I would be very grateful indeed if you could spare me some of your time to share some of your expert knowledge, but I fully understand that this may not be possible.
> Thank you for taking the time to read this letter.
> Yours sincerely
>
> B. Palmer
>
> Brian Palmer

Figure 4.1 A student's letter inviting a participant to take part in research

ACTIVITY

Identify one person who has particular expertise related to your project. This could be someone at your local university, the author of a book you have read, or a businessman, artist or academic working in the particular field of your EP. Check that you have their correct name, title and postal address, then write them a letter about your proposed EP. Do not assume that they will be able to help you, but there are many people who will be delighted to share their interests and experience with you.

Before you write to anyone, check with your EP supervisor about your school's or college's safeguarding policy. This will affect what information you can provide to the person receiving your letter. Do *not* use your personal e-mail account or your home address. Keep your supervisor informed about any communication that you receive.

Experiments

If you decide to conduct an experiment involving human research participants, think carefully about how you will select your participants. Have you considered the ethics of your research (see Appendix 2)? How many participants will you involve? Where and when will the experiment take place? Will there be a control group? How will you ensure that any data collected is reliable? Do not fall into the trap of asking a few of your friends to participate in your experiment and then generalising the results from your experiment in a way that cannot be justified. Your friends may have opinions, biases or characteristics that are not shared by the wider population you are investigating.

Example

Jade is investigating the suggestion that listening to music can improve cognitive function and in particular short-term memory. She intends to ask 18 of her friends to play a version of 'Kim's game'. In this game, a tray of objects is shown to a participant for 30 seconds. The tray is then removed and the participant is given 60 seconds to write down as many of the objects as they can remember. Nine of the friends will play the game in silence. The other nine will play the game with music composed by Mozart playing in the background.

The following questions should be answered before Jade proceeds:

- All of Jade's friends are of the same age. Does this matter? What implications might this fact have on her investigation?
- Jade has not considered gender differences. Is this relevant? What implications might this fact have on her investigation?
- Why has Jade decided to allocate nine participants to play the game in silence and the other nine to play the game listening to music by Mozart? What research relating to sample size has she undertaken?
- Will the game be played by all participants in the same place at the same time of day? Will there be one participant per day for 18 days? Or 18 separate experiments on the same day? How many trays of identical objects does Jade have? Will she have friends helping her gather her data?
- Has Jade considered the environment in which the game will be played? Might there be distractions, other than the music, that could affect the results?
- Will each participant be shown exactly the same set of objects displayed in exactly the same way?
- Has Jade considered the statistical analysis she intends to undertake having gathered her data?
- Might it be more worthwhile to run the full experiment with all eighteen friends playing the game twice, with two trays of different objects, but once with music and once without? (Jade has read that paired experiments are more powerful, but organising this as a matched pairs experiment would be very complicated.)
- Has Jade considered the ethics involved with her experiment? Has she explained her research, gained informed consent, and assured her participants about confidentiality and anonymity? Do her participants understand their right to withdraw?
- Has Jade considered other possible tasks for her research participants other than 'Kim's game'?
- Has Jade searched thoroughly for write-ups of similar research?

To collect primary data from an experiment it is very important to set up the experiment in such a way that any differences in outcomes can clearly be attributed to the specific factor you are testing. You should also consider which form of statistical analysis will be appropriate for your experiment *before* deciding to undertake the experiment (see Appendix 3).

4 Resources

TIP

If you do not feel confident in your understanding of appropriate statistical analysis, you can *either* decide not to include data collection that requires such analysis *or* do research into appropriate use of statistics as part of your EPQ research.

Sometimes EPQ students conduct a small-scale experiment that produces results that are not reliable. In retrospect, the students have understood too late that their time might have been better spent searching for examples of data gathered by undergraduates or postgraduates conducting similar experiments on a larger scale. Before deciding to undertake any form of time-consuming primary research it is always worth looking to see if similar data has already been collected and published.

If you decide to make use of data gathered by another researcher, however, carefully check out their methodology and only use data that is reliable.

Appendix 3 includes some suggestions to help you choose appropriate statistical analysis methods, should you need them.

Questionnaires

If you decide to create and use a questionnaire as part of your research, think carefully about how to select your participants. Will the questionnaire responses truly represent the population that you are investigating? What steps will you take to select participants without an in-built bias? When selecting participants, what type of sampling technique will you employ? How will you decide on the size of your sample? Will it be fair to generalise based on your collected data? See Appendix 3 for details relating to sampling techniques.

ACTIVITY

Freya is a member of a women's rugby team. For her EP she is researching the use of artificial additives in British confectionery. She creates a questionnaire and takes 20 copies of it with her to her next rugby match. She asks ten players from each team to complete it. Freya intends to use the data gathered from these 20 questionnaires to represent the opinion of the British public towards the use of artificial additives in food.

List as many reasons as you can that suggest Freya's data may not be a fair representation of the opinions of the British adult population.

TIP

It will rarely be the case that a questionnaire handed out to your friends and family will generate much worthwhile data unless your EP topic is itself focused particularly on an issue that specifically relates to your friends and family.

Suppose you want to research the attitudes of 18-year-old girls, for example. You may have access to many 18-year-old girls from your school and college, but they probably all come from just one area in the UK. Random sampling from across your whole school or college would be better than just asking your friends to complete your questionnaire, but even then your sample would represent only your school's or college's 18-year-olds. It cannot be said to represent the UK's 18-year-old girls.

The design of a questionnaire takes time and care. It is easy to write a misleading or confusing question. A question might seem straightforward to you, but you are writing it with knowledge that the respondents may not have. Making sure that your questions are clear and unambiguous may take you some time. Questions should be in grammatically correct English. Avoid asking emotive or leading questions, such as 'Using animals to test cosmetics is wrong. Do you agree?'

You have the opportunity to ask:

- **closed** questions, in which the respondent has a limited number of choices. For example:
  - Were you born in the UK? Yes/No
  - How would you rate the taste of the biscuit on a scale of 1 to 10, where 1 means 'very delicious' and 10 means 'not at all delicious'?
- **open** questions, which have no limits and require the respondent to express their response in words of their own. For example:
  - Why did you stop eating meat?
  - What could be done to improve the inclusion of minorities in this school?

Too many open questions might be off-putting to a questionnaire respondent. But if all questions are closed, respondents may feel that they haven't had a chance to express their opinion. A balance is required.

TIP

Think carefully before deciding to include questionnaire design and use as part of your EP. How valuable is the data likely to be? Will this be a good use of your time?

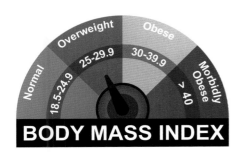

ACTIVITY

Sky has written a set of six questions designed to find out if the amount of exercise taken by students at her school is related to their BMI.

1 *What is your full name?* _____
2 *How many times did you exercise last week? 1/2/3/4/more than 4 (circle one)*
3 *What is your BMI?* _____
4 *What sports do you play?* _____
5 *How old are you? 10–12/12–14/14–16/over 16 (circle one)*
6 *Do your parents exercise regularly? Yes/No (circle one)*

How could Sky's questionnaire be improved?

ACTIVITY

Imagine that you intend to use SurveyMonkey to gain opinion from 100 residents of your village about a proposed new village hall. You have selected your 100 participants carefully to represent a complete cross-section of the village population. Seventy responses come back to you.

Why might gathering information in this way not truly represent a complete cross-section of the residents of your village?

An advantage of handing out questionnaires to be completed by the research participants in private is that you avoid the risk of 'interviewer bias'. Responses from participants on an anonymous questionnaire will be less affected by the fact that it is *you* asking the questions. Anonymous questionnaires also reduce the possibility that some participants may give the response that they believe you *want* to hear. For example, it is less likely in a face-to-face interview situation that overtly discriminatory opinion will be expressed, but such opinion may be discovered, if it exists, in an anonymous questionnaire.

It is possible to use internet sites such as www.surveymonkey.com to deliver questionnaires online. SurveyMonkey allows you to create a questionnaire with up to 10 questions and gather responses from up to 100 respondents free of charge. Please note, however, that even if the responses are anonymous it is important that *you* know who your respondents are, otherwise you will not be able to analyse how representative they are of the target population that you are studying.

Would structured or unstructured interviews be more useful for your project?

Interviews

You may decide to include some interviews as part of your research. Before asking someone to become part of your research in this way, you should subject them to the same level of scrutiny as any other resource. Do not assume that someone will have expert knowledge, check their credentials for yourself. Where were they educated? What has been their career path? Are they recognised as being authoritative by their peers? Similarly, if you interview someone as a representative of a certain group or population, be mindful that their opinions may not be the same as those of other members of that group.

Once you are convinced that you have selected an appropriate interviewee, prepare carefully for your interview. An interview is a guided conversation and you, the interviewer, must be well-prepared to guide the conversation effectively. When booking the interview think carefully about the chosen time and place. You will need to have quiet and privacy. Consider the ethics of your proposed interview and carry out a risk assessment (see Appendices 1 and 2). Wear appropriate clothing for the interview and be very polite.

In some cases an interview will be a face-to-face completion of a questionnaire. Often researchers will distribute questionnaires and ask research participants to complete them in private and return them, but you may prefer to sit with each research participant, to read out the questions and write down their responses yourself. The advantage of collecting data in this way is that questions can be explained to your participants, if required. The disadvantage, of course, is that it will take up much more of your time. Interviews of this type are called **structured** and involve mostly closed questions. You ask exactly the same questions to each interviewee. Generally, this type of interview is used to gather quantitative data. Once you have gathered data of this type you will be able to analyse it using various statistical measures (see Appendix 3).

Interviews that are **unstructured** are generally used by researchers seeking qualitative data. Interviews of this type will be much more chatty and conversational. They enable a researcher to learn about the beliefs, opinions and attitudes of the participants. Thematic analysis is very time-consuming, however. It is much harder to effectively analyse data of this nature. You need to look for repeated or dominant themes and it is essential to remain objective, giving all responses equal attention. The use of a word cloud can help with the analysis of such data, this use is discussed in Appendix 3.

Probably the most common form of interview is **semi-structured**. The interviewer includes a mix of closed and open questions. The closed questions can gather quantitative data efficiently, and the interviewer has flexibility to also gather some qualitative data.

If you intend to make an audio recording of an interview you must seek permission from your interviewee beforehand. You must also build in time for the subsequent transcription of this recording, making using interviews a time-consuming option. Researchers using interviews within their research frequently pay for transcription to be undertaken professionally, but it is unlikely that you will have the funds available to employ a professional transcription service. Ask yourself whether the time you would need to spend transcribing interviews would be a good use of your EP time and how much the interview evidence would add to your body of research.

There are various things you should consider carefully before any interview:

- Is the interviewee clear about the purpose of the interview?
- Have you carefully explained what you are investigating?
- Is the scope of the interview clearly defined?
- How long will the interview last and have you made your expectation of interview duration clear to the interviewee?
- Are you clear about how you will spend the interview time?

Estimate carefully the time required for each response, do not waste time on chit-chat and avoid irrelevant discussions. Have questions that lead on from certain responses written out and ready to ask, even if they are not actually used. It is a good idea to start an interview with a neutral question to settle the interviewee in. Limit the focus of each question to a single idea, to avoid any ambiguity or confusion. Do not ask leading or emotive questions, do not present your own opinion, do not pass any judgements (including through facial expressions). Be prepared to ask an interviewee to repeat an answer if you have not fully understood or captured their response.

ACTIVITY

Identify one person who is an expert in the area of your EP.

- Write a set of interview questions for this expert.
- Include both closed and open questions.
- Estimate how long you should allow for this interview.
- Ask a friend to act in the place of your expert and conduct a 'mock' interview.
- Produce a full transcription of the mock interview.

How long did the mock interview take? How good was your estimate? Were there any questions that did not produce sensible answers? If so, was it because your friend is not an expert in the area of your EP, or was the question itself flawed? How long did it take you to write up the transcription?

TIP

It is important to include transcriptions of any interviews that you do. Give details about the date, location and duration of the interview. Within your report you can then directly cite from the transcription.

Sometimes you may be able to conduct interviews by videocall or telephone. By whatever means an interview is conducted, at the end of the interview give a brief summary of the interview responses and ask the interviewee if this is an accurate record. Remember to thank interviewees and remind them once again that they have the right to withdraw their responses, and that these will remain anonymous and confidential.

If you are considering the use of interviews as part of your research to gain qualitative data on opinions or beliefs, it would be worth reading a research paper entitled 'How many interviews are enough? An experiment with data saturation and variability' by Guest, Bunce and Johnson. They found that at least twelve interviews are required from separate members of a target population to reach what is called 'theoretical saturation' (the point at which no new information or themes are brought out via interview responses). What this means for your EP is that if you interview fewer than twelve representatives of the group that interests you then this is not likely to provide information that can reliably be said to represent the group.

Piloting

Whether you are doing an experiment, issuing a questionnaire or embarking on a series of interviews, a very important step in the process is 'piloting', which involves some form of trial or mock-up of the intended activity.

Example

Emily is doing an EP looking at the value of a particular approach to early years education, known as the 'Forest School' approach. As part of her research she prepares two questionnaires, one designed for completion by practitioners working in the education of children aged under 5 years, the other for parents of children of this age.

Emily asks three parents and three practitioners to complete her pilot questionnaires and to provide feedback.

From this small pilot Emily is able to discover that some questions were not sufficiently clear and that others provided little worthwhile data. She amends her questionnaires in light of these pilot responses and feedback.

Emily is now able to distribute her improved questionnaires with confidence that they are clear and should produce responses that will be valuable to her research.

It is important to have 'trial runs' of experiments, questionnaires and interviews so that any weaknesses in the original planning can be dealt with before the 'real' experiments, questionnaires or interviews take place. You should write in your Log about your piloting and the changes (if any) that you have made as a result of your pilot.

Secondary sources

Most books and journals that you use will be secondary sources and include, for example, historical accounts of past events. Writing that refers to primary sources and data is a secondary source. By using secondary sources, you will be able to benefit from the time and effort put in by the author of the secondary source. In many cases a secondary source will itself have been produced as the result of painstaking research.

Example

John is a keen cyclist and a fan of the Tour de Yorkshire. John decides to observe the full four days of the 2018 race from various places on the route. He decides to keep an audio diary using a small hand-held audio recorder. John records all his observations of the four-day race. Later in the year John is approached by Ivy, a journalist for a local newspaper. Ivy has been asked to write an article about the Tour de Yorkshire and has been told about John's audio diary. John willingly shares his recording with Ivy and she uses this to write her article. John's audio diary, all 18 hours of it, is a primary source. It is a first-hand account of direct observation of the race.

Ivy's article is a secondary source. She has included information provided by John, but she did not herself see the race. Ivy is probably writing her article with a particular audience in mind, and there will be some underlying theme even if it is not immediately obvious.

Note, however, that if you are undertaking an EP related to the Tour de Yorkshire, it is unlikely that you will have time available to spend 18 hours listening to the primary data. It may be a better use of your time to read Ivy's article.

When using any secondary source, you should always be cautious. Inevitably all authors have opinions, beliefs and personal bias that will affect the conclusions they draw when considering an issue or event. You may also be reading an interpretation of an event made by someone who was not actually present at the time of the event. You may be aware of the way that politicians representing different political parties can take the same raw data and interpret it in significantly different ways. This is true to a greater or lesser extent in most academic disciplines.

There are very few areas of secondary research where you will not encounter opinion. Even in scientific literature conclusions are sometimes drawn with hidden assumptions that particular laws or theories are in fact 'true'. If you dig a little deeper you will sometimes find that a law or theory is accepted without conclusive proof because it currently offers the best model to help us understand the world or universe. The law or theory is presented as an acceptable underlying assumption. As new evidence emerges and science develops, the old hidden assumptions may be replaced by new ones.

As an extreme example consider the time of Copernicus, when scholars influenced by the Catholic Church believed that the sun moved around the Earth and not vice versa. This belief affected interpretations of raw data, and to suggest that the Earth was *not* the centre of the universe was very dangerous at that time. Galileo, developing the ideas of Copernicus, was found guilty of heresy in 1633 for his insistence that the Earth revolved around the sun.

An example of theories changing is seen in the very different treatment of soldiers with post-traumatic stress disorder today, compared to the treatment of soldiers returning from the First World War. During the First World War this disorder was called 'shell shock'. As more evidence has been gathered, theories and hence treatments related to this type of trauma have changed and developed. (Note, however, that there will always be differing interpretations of the same evidence and not all conclusions drawn by experts working in this particular field of study today are identical.)

Initial reading

It is usual for a student undertaking the EPQ to begin their research by reading some carefully selected secondary sources. This reading may then provide ideas for further research including both primary and secondary sources. The bibliography within a secondary source is often a good place to find further secondary sources.

Reading secondary literature for your EP may also suggest some potential primary data collection that you could do.

Example

Ming is interested in the use of good hygiene to reduce the spread of transmissible diseases. She starts her research by reading an article published in the *Indian Journal of Medical Research* entitled 'Hand hygiene: Back to the basics of infection control'. From the bibliography, she finds an article from the US National Library of Medicine entitled 'Epidemiologic background of hand hygiene and evaluation of the most important agents for scrubs and rubs'. This article is complicated but her interest becomes focused on different approaches to handwashing as a means of controlling infection.

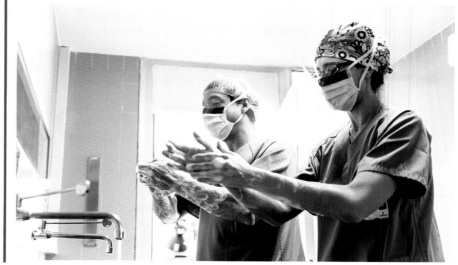

Ming decides that her EP offers her a great opportunity: she can design and undertake primary research related to handwashing. She designs an experiment using research participants to see for herself how the quality of handwashing and type of soap used affects the cleanliness of hands. Ming would like to use her EP to allow her to develop her practical laboratory skills.

Ming also decides that her EP would benefit from input from health professionals. She will contact a family friend who works as a nurse in a large NHS hospital. If she is lucky this friend will agree to be interviewed.

Eventually Ming may decide to use only sources from the UK, so the first two resources referred to above may not form part of her bibliography. Ming will still refer to them in her Log, however, because she understands that she must provide evidence to show how her resources were selected.

Using an up-to-date, reputable encyclopedia can be a good place to start your research. There are many such encyclopedia available. For example, your school or college may have a subscription to the online Encyclopedia Britannica. You may also begin your research online with careful use of Wikipedia.

Don't listen to anyone who dismisses all use of Wikipedia as 'wicked'. Most articles found on the site have been written by recognised experts. There is always, however, the possibility that an article on Wikipedia contains incorrect information. Wikipedia is not as rigorously edited and checked as, say, the Encyclopedia Britannica, but Wikipedia is free to use and easy to access. Reading an entry from Wikipedia may give you a good overview of a topic, but you should check out all the references from the article carefully. You should not include any citations directly from a Wikipedia page in your EP. Use the bibliography of Wikipedia articles to lead you to articles in other published sources that can be referenced in your EP.

Later in this chapter we will discuss evaluation of sources. Provided you scrutinise Wikipedia articles rigorously there is no reason to dismiss them and some may provide you with worthwhile research leads. Any Wikipedia articles that have no references, however, should be treated with great caution.

How to use a library for research

Libraries will usually provide you with access to online materials, newspapers, magazines, books, journals and various other valuable resources. Most towns and cities have a public library that you will be able to join. You may have a school or college library that you can use and you may also be granted access to your local university library. Whichever libraries you decide to use, learning how to use them efficiently is a great skill to develop, especially if you intend to enrol on a course of higher education.

ACTIVITY

Using either an online encyclopedia or an encyclopedia from a library (it is also fine to use Wikipedia), look up a topic that relates to your EP. Use the references and links to find a minimum of three resources that might be useful as you embark on your EP.

> **TIP**
>
> When using libraries, do not be afraid to ask for help from the librarians. They are the experts here!

Libraries are staffed by librarians and it is usually a librarian who will provide you with an induction into how a particular library is organised. The reading, listening or viewing material will be stored according to a system. You need to learn the system. Usually there will be numbered stacks of bookshelves arranged broadly by subject area, with individual sections of books arranged alphabetically by author. There may also be drawers containing potential research materials. Every item in the library will have been carefully catalogued and identified by a unique code. The first skill you need to master is how to use the cataloguing system and then you need to learn how to interpret the code. These two skills will enable you to locate the books and other research materials that the library offers.

Most libraries have an electronic database for the majority of their items, but there are some libraries that still use a physical index-card system, perhaps only for special collections and archive items. Some libraries will grant you access to their online catalogue so you do not need to travel to the library to use the catalogue. Your online browsing of the library's resources can be done at home or school so that your trip to the library can be used to find and examine the items that you have identified from the catalogue as being of potential interest.

The use of the catalogue will be explained to you by the librarian, as will the best way to search for relevant items. It is always worth asking if there might be materials in an archive or special collection that you would be allowed to access.

Generally, you will need to have key search words ready when trying to find relevant research materials. The more focused your search words, the more likely it is that you will be able to find items relevant for your EP. This is also true for any internet searches that you undertake.

Librarians will also explain to you the laws and regulations relating to photocopying and copyright. Having been granted access to borrow an item from a library does not automatically mean that you have the right to copy pages from it, and this should be checked carefully before you rush to use the library's photocopier.

Using the internet for research

The boundless nature of the internet makes it a very valuable place to undertake research. At the same time its enormity and diversity should make you very cautious when trying to find research material. There are many sites that contain *unreliable* information. The internet is not controlled and 'information' may not be factually correct.

Your school or college may recommend that you use particular search engines or news services because they have been evaluated and deemed to be suitable and reliable. Here is a list of sites that may be of use to you, depending on your chosen EP. Have a look at these to see what they offer. Note that information found through these links has not been through the AQA approval process.

- books.google.co.uk and various other sites such as http://archive.org and www.smashwords.com offer a wealth of free ebooks. Sites like these are of particular use if you are studying in a school or college with limited opportunities to visit a library.
- http://completeissues.co.uk (created by Carel Press Ltd) offers a range of carefully selected resources focusing on topic areas chosen because they are of interest and concern to young people.
- http://creativecommons.org offers you the possibility of using work from artists and academics within your EP. The site contains songs, videos, scientific and academic articles, all of which can be freely and legally used under the terms of the creative commons copyright licences.
- http://credoreference.com is a commercial online reference collection. It contains over 900 online encyclopedias, subject dictionaries, biographical resources and reference tools.
- http://doaj.org (the Directory of Open Access Journals) provides free access to peer-reviewed academic journals.
- http://explore.bl.uk is a website that contains the catalogue of the British Library, including millions of records for books, journals, newspapers, printed maps, musical scores, electronic resources and sound archive items. You will not be able to access everything that is catalogued but there are thousands of open-access items freely available online.
- www.flickr.com/commons contains photographs that are available to use under one of the creative commons licences. The photographer owns the copyright, but you may use them so long as you abide by the licence terms.
- www.gutenberg.org is a site frequently used by students of the EPQ. It offers free access to more than 50,000 ebooks.
- **iTunes U** is a section of Apple's iTunes music store and enables you to download a range of educational audio and video files from universities, museums and other organisations.
- www.jstor.com is a digital library that includes thousands of academic journals, books and primary source documents. Accessing it requires a subscription — your school or college may have a subscription to Jstor.
- http://morguefile.com is another website database, particularly useful for students seeking photographs for their EP.
- www.questia.com is an online commercial digital library of books and academic articles with a particular emphasis on the humanities and social sciences. It is often used by students of the EPQ working in schools or colleges that are not close to a university.
- scholar.google.co.uk is free to access and offers a simple way to search online for scholarly literature. You can search for articles, theses,

books, abstracts, etc., from academic publishers, professional societies, universities and other organisations. Note, however, that your searches may only give you access to the abstracts (short summaries) of journal articles. Not all information is free to access. You may need to access full articles via a university library.

- www.ted.com is a source frequently used by EPQ students seeking short lectures on specific subjects or given by selected speakers.
- http://vimeo.com contains thousands of videos that have been shared by their creators. The 'royalty free' section may be of especial use should you be seeking to incorporate video extracts into an artefact.

ACTIVITY

Choose five of the internet sites listed above and find at least one resource from each that might offer valuable research material for your EP. For each resource conduct a *full* evaluation, as internet resources require careful scrutiny.

- Check that there is an identifiable author. If an author cannot be identified you will not be able to fully reference the source, neither will you know if the piece is written by a credible expert.
- Is there a named editor who has checked and verified any information included in the resource?
- Check that all stated 'facts' are referenced so their origin can be verified.

- Is this online resource sponsored by an organisation or commercial enterprise? Might it therefore have commercial, political or religious bias? Is there any advertising?
- Are there contact details given for the resource that can be checked, such as names, postal addresses or telephone numbers? Look for an 'About us' link.
- Check the URL (web address) of the resource.
- Is the resource dated? Is the information up to date? Are you able to follow links? Dead links suggest that a page has not been updated.
- Is the information relevant for your EP?

ACTIVITY

Zac is undertaking an EP on the innovative use of modern technology in schools. He comes across the use of 'digital surgeries' as a means to help young people engage in politics by allowing them to talk directly via videocall to local and national politicians. On the internet he finds the 2017 Impact Report on the pilot scheme for such surgeries, run by an organisation called The Politics Project.

Should Zac trust that this report contains factually correct information?

- Look for named politicians who have been cited in the report. Could they be contacted for direct verification?
- Do the schools listed in the report all exist? Could they be contacted for direct verification?
- Follow the 'About us' link. Does this organisation have reputable sponsors?
- What else could Zac do to feel confident that he can trust the information contained in this report?

Evaluation of resources

Before making any use of a resource that you have found, it is vital that you evaluate it and establish it is a **relevant** resource that will be able to provide you with **reliable** information. In your Log, explain why you have chosen to use — or not use — the resources that you have considered. Every resource should be **selected** and **evaluated** with care.

For any published piece of writing, be it a book, online article, newspaper report or academic paper, there are several key questions that you should be asking *before* you select this piece of writing for inclusion as part of your research.

First of all, you should consider the author. Are they an expert in your chosen field? What is their education and career history? You may find it useful to apply an acronym that is used in critical thinking: **RAVEN**.

R **Reputation:** Is the author writing for a publication or publishing house that is recognised as being authoritative and impartial, or does it have a reputation for putting forward particular political views? If the publication is a journal, is this journal one in which respected academics publish their research reports?

 Example

Charlie is intending to use an article published in *Nature*. She should have no difficulty finding information about this weekly scientific journal to assure her of its very high reputation within the scientific community.

A **Ability to observe:** Is the author writing from first-hand experience?

If an event is being written by someone who was not themselves an observer of the event, they may exaggerate or distort the facts. This is because they may not have fully understood the description of the event, or they may have underlying beliefs and opinions that influence their writing. Be aware, however, that the personal beliefs and opinions of a direct observer of an event can also affect what they see. For example, consider the directly observed evidence from the fans of opposing teams at football matches. Was it a foul? Was it a fair tackle?

Example

On 22 November 1963, newspaper reporter Hugh Aynesworth was an eyewitness to the assassination of President Kennedy. Articles written by this reporter therefore have the benefit of his direct observation of events, unlike many other contemporary articles that drew on other people's descriptions of what they saw.

Aynesworth became the lead reporter of the story at the *Dallas Morning News*.

V **Vested Interest:** Is the author, or more likely the person paying them to write the book or article, trying to 'sell' a particular point of view? Be aware of potential commercial influence.

Example

Paula has decided to investigate the potential benefit to her mother's farm were the family to build a small-scale hydroelectricity system in a stream flowing through their land. She finds some really helpful information on the HydroElec website. It may be appropriate for Paula to make use of this information, but HydroElec is a business and Paula should check carefully that the claims it makes about the costs, output and efficiency of its pumps have not been exaggerated.

E **Expertise:** Do not allow letters after someone's name, on their own, to convince you that they are an expert in the area you are investigating. If possible, take time to check an author's career and qualifications. Also check the credentials of any 'expert' cited by an author in a book or article.

Example

George is researching for his EP about adoption laws in the UK. He finds an article in the *Guardian* newspaper from June 2017 discussing the legal aspects of adoption.

Alice Noon, the head of adoption at the Coram Foundation, was cited in the *Guardian* report. Can Noon be considered an expert in the field of adoption? How can George find this out? A quick internet search tells George that Noon has been working for Coram since 2009. Coram runs one of the largest and most successful independent adoption agencies in the UK. Thus George can feel confident that the citations attributed to Noon in the article can be trusted as expert opinion related to adoption laws.

N **Neutrality or bias:** Is there anything influencing the author? For example strong feelings about religion, feminism, animal rights, etc. Who was the intended audience when the piece was written? Does the author use emotive language or make unreferenced assertions?

Do not dismiss a resource as being biased just because the author is writing on a particular side of a debate, but be aware of the *possibility* of bias. Before rejecting a resource due to bias, be sure that you have found evidence of bias within the resource. Is the author distorting the facts? Is the author deliberately attempting to mislead the reader? Are assertions being made that are not backed up by verified evidence? In certain circumstances, it might be appropriate to include an overtly biased resource if you are doing research into opinions rather than facts. You may then seek a similarly biased resource putting forward an opposing stance.

 Example

Andrew is undertaking an EP related to President Trump's decision to reduce environmental review requirements for major infrastructure projects in the USA. He finds several newspaper articles that cite a person called Kym Hunter. He undertakes a search and discovers that since 2010 Hunter has worked as an Attorney at the Chapel Hill Office of the Southern Environmental Law Center (SELC), a non-profit organisation with a mission to 'strengthen environmental protection laws and policies'. Hunter's credentials include a first-class degree in Environmental Studies from the University of East Anglia (UK) and Doctor of Law (JD) from Georgetown University (USA). Her career includes work at the Georgetown Climate Centre and internships with Earthjustice and the Environmental Law Institute.

Andrew has no doubts about Hunter's expertise, but thinks he should be cautious when reading articles written by her. She will clearly be taking a pro-environment stance in her approach to environmental review. Andrew should try to balance his research by also including articles from authors who look at the review stages preceding the construction of major infrastructure projects from a different perspective.

Other questions that you should be asking yourself when evaluating your potential resources include:

- Has the author referenced their work thoroughly (just as you should be referencing your own EP report)? It is a good idea to check out some of the citations found within the writing. If the author is citing resources that themselves appear to be unreliable then this will probably not be a resource you should trust.
- If the piece of writing is itself a research report, what methodology did the author use? Does the chosen methodology allow for valid conclusions to be drawn? (See Appendix 3 for some examples of ways in which data might be collected and analysed.)
- Has this piece of writing been 'peer reviewed'? Are there endorsements of the piece of writing from other established experts in the research area? For example, if it is an article written about research on the long-term success of dental implants, has this piece of writing been read and favourably commented on by independent experts in this field of dentistry?
- Is the material contained here relevant for your project? For example, do not use statistics relating to crime in the USA if your project is focused on crime in the UK.
- When was the resource written? Will the information that it provides still be relevant and true? For example, a book on fashion trends in London that was written in 1963 will not be relevant if your EP on fashion trends in London is focused on the 1990s. For other EP topics, however, it may be very sensible to see how opinions/interpretations of findings have changed over time, and for these topics ignoring older publications might result in the omission of relevant research material.

ACTIVITY

Consider this book. Why should you trust this as an authority with respect to the EPQ?

One reason is that Hodder Education is a respected publisher of educational literature. Also, this book has been approved by AQA, a respected examination board. To dig deeper, consider the following questions:

- Who is the author and what are her credentials?
- When was the book published?
- Has it been revised?
- Is the information contained likely to be up-to-date?
- Check out some of the resources suggested by the author. Do they still exist?

Considering all this information together, do you think this book is a trustworthy source of information on the EPQ?

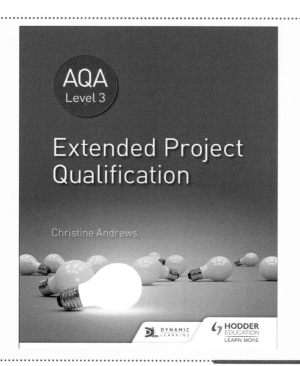

Think about possible bias when using secondary sources

Potential resources for your EP should be carefully scrutinised *before* you begin to make use of them. Within your EP submission — either in your Log, your report, your presentation or in some form of appendix — you should provide evidence of the careful selection and evaluation process that you have used to establish a wide, relevant and reliable set of resources.

ACTIVITY

For each of the resources that you have so far identified for your EP, answer as many of the following questions as you can:

- Is the publisher reputable?
- What are the author's credentials? Most books should provide biographical information on the author, but an internet search may also help.
- If this is a journal article, has it been peer reviewed? Articles that are published in popular magazines are less likely to have been subjected to peer review.
- When was the resource published? Is it an earlier publication that has been revised and updated? For scientific research, it is likely that you will require recently published or revised material.
- Who is the intended audience for this piece of writing? For example, BBC Bitesize is aimed at students studying for GCSEs and it is unlikely that it could provide research of sufficient depth for your EP.
- Does the piece of writing offer fact or opinion? Beware skilled writers who write persuasively and offer you their interpretation of 'facts'.
- Does the author support their writing with evidence that is clearly referenced? You will be doing this when you write the report for your EP.
- Are there any uses of emotive language by the author or is the piece objective and impartial throughout?

Resource evaluation tables

You may find using a table like Table 4.1 helpful when evaluating resources, but do not fall into the trap of cutting and pasting set phrases into the columns. Each resource that you use should be fully scrutinised, but in some cases you may not be able to fill in every column. Some example comments have been included in the table on page 62. Do not copy these. Use your own words and make your own judgements. Use of a 'resource evaluation table' is not a requirement of the specification: you can provide evidence of your selection and evaluation of resources in whatever way suits you.

Table 4.1 A resource evaluation table

Title	Resource type	Author	(Author) credentials	Publisher	Publisher credentials	Date of publication	Relevance of resource	Interested parties	Intended audience	Peer review	Methodology employed	Well referenced/ author opinion	Should I use this source?
More Mathematical Activities	Book	Brian Bolt	Worked at School of Education, Exeter University	Cambridge University Press	CUP is trusted	1985	Lots of puzzles, I am looking for puzzles for my artefact	N/A	Teachers	None found	N/A	N/A	Yes, a valuable source
The Story of Art	Book	E.H. Gombrich	Highly valued Professor of Fine Art	Phaidon Press, Oxford	Renowned publisher of the creative arts	First, 1950; this impression 1982	Section on the 18th century is of relevance	N/A	Teenagers and adults seeking to understand the world of art	Professor Jansen from New York University	Story-telling, educating	Location of every piece of artwork given Interpretation of artwork is largely author opinion	Yes, but it would be wise to find alternative scholars' opinions to compare
Andrew Collins	Person	N/A	Works in purchasing department of major supermarket chain	N/A	N/A	N/A	Has first-hand experience of supermarket purchasing policies	May be biased either towards or against his employer	N/A	Andrew was recommended by a colleague as a potential interviewee	I will use a semi-structured interview	I will ask Andrew to suggest avenues of further research	Yes, record the interview
People's History Museum	Museum	N/A	Highly acclaimed Focuses on development of democracy in Britain	N/A	N/A	Opened in present location in 1990 Origins date back to 1960s	Trade union archive materials Perfect for my EP	It has no political affiliation but be cautious	All ages	Has received many positive reviews	Primary research	Be ready to ask archivists to help interpret materials	Yes, get an appointment booked

Triangulation

When a secondary source provides facts, figures and dates, you should try and find an independently written resource to check this information. This checking is referred to as 'triangulation'. If authors are not in factual agreement, why would you believe one author more than another? For example, when undertaking research into aspects of the politics or history of a foreign country it may be hard to find independent resources that you can trust. Authors writing about the country from outside will be reliant on interpretations of events from second-hand reports. Authors writing from within the country may have been subject to censorship. If there is significant factual disagreement between authors it may be wise to reconsider your EP topic.

Triangulation is also important if you decide to include primary research. Use secondary sources to compare with the primary data that you have collected.

 Example

Jen is planning to create an artefact. She is undertaking research that will enable her to create a teacher pack on astronomy for use in Key Stage 2. As part of her research Jen interviews her aunt, who is a teacher of children in her local primary school. Jen understands, however, that she must also undertake secondary research using books and articles written by recognised experts in the field of Key Stage 2 education. She may well find that the advice and suggestions provided by her aunt are reinforced by the secondary research, but if she does not she will have to think carefully about why the information coming from her different resources is not in agreement.

Be careful when looking for triangulation between secondary sources that a source is not referencing the source that you are trying to check. You want to find, if possible, independent corroboration of factual information.

Relative value of resources

Before you make your final selection of resources, look carefully at the range of resources that are possibly relevant to your EP.

- How many of them involve primary research?
- Will any primary data that you hope to gather be quantitative or qualitative?
- How do you intend to collect and analyse your primary data?
- Estimate how much time it will take you to undertake each piece of potential research.

When selecting the best resources for your EP you will have to ask yourself about their relative value to you as the researcher. Sometimes students devote lots of time to primary research that provides little reliable data. These students may have spent very little time on wider secondary research. When planning your EP it is important to estimate the time that any proposed primary data collection may take and how reliable and relevant the data you intend to collect is likely to be, *before* deciding to embark on the data collection. Will the proposed primary research generate data that can genuinely inform your project?

Do not think that primary data will be wholly reliable because you collected it directly. An important feature of reliable primary research is that it can be replicated by other researchers. Ask yourself whether a different researcher gathering primary data using the same methodology as you is likely to collect the same (or very similar) data. If you think that it is unlikely to be the same (or very similar) you should consider how reliable the data is. If the data is not reliable, how far will you be able to use it as a base from which to draw conclusions?

TIP

Many successful EPs involve research that is exclusively from secondary sources. This is perfectly acceptable — the choice of type of resource to use is entirely yours. Do not feel that you will produce a less worthy EP if you choose not to include primary research.

CHECKLIST

Do I understand:

- [ ] the huge variety of potential EP resources?
- [ ] the difference between primary and secondary sources?
- [ ] how to be meticulous in my approach to research involving people?
- [ ] how to pilot questionnaires, interviews and experiments?
- [ ] how to approach research by using libraries and/or the internet?
- [ ] what is required of me when I evaluate a resource?
- [ ] how to triangulate my resource material?
- [ ] how to estimate the potential value of resources for my EP?

5

Developing your project

Documenting project progress

So far you have:

- considered initial ideas and formulated a project proposal
- had your proposal approved (with or without recommendations from your centre coordinator)
- created a Project Plan with clear aims and SMART objectives
- learnt how to select and evaluate resources for your project and established a good set of reliable resources as a base from which to commence your research

It is time for you to commence your research in earnest, telling the story of each stage of your project journey in your Production Log.

What you should record in your Production Log

Sometimes students of the EPQ ask about their Log: 'Why does it matter? Surely all that matters is the product that I will eventually produce?' But you need to remember that the EPQ is different to other qualifications, in that it is a qualification based on process. In the EPQ what is important is the **evidenced development** of high-level skills.

By completing the Production Log you will provide evidence of:

- skill development and use
- decision-making
- thought and reflection

If you study the criteria by which your EP will be judged you will see that evidence of decision-making and reflection plays a significant role (see Appendix 5 for the AQA criteria). Keeping a detailed Log is crucial, even if it sometimes seems less important than your other work.

The **Record of Initial Ideas** page of the Log provides some evidence of your thinking and decision-making as you considered different project ideas. The **Planning Review** page shows your development of planning and project management skills. (See Chapters 2 and 3 for more details of these pages of the Log.)

The next page that you will complete in your Log will be the **Mid-project Review** page. This should not be written until you have completed the research phase of your project. In the Mid-project Review you will have the opportunity to discuss and reflect on the development of your Project Plan, justifying your choices of resources and research methodologies.

The pages of the Log provide evidence of your problem-solving, decision-making and creative thinking as your EP develops. Anyone reading your Log should have a good understanding of what you are aiming to achieve, the objectives you have set to achieve your aims, the methodologies and resources you have decided to use, and why you have chosen to use them. You should make reference to the ups and downs of your EP journey. Refer to any problems or disappointments encountered and explain how you overcame them.

Try not to write entries in your Log that give no explanation or reasoning, such as 'I have dropped the idea of using questionnaire data.' This example gives no evidence to explain *why* you took this decision. Try instead to write entries that explain your actions: 'I have decided to abandon my initial idea of collecting questionnaire data because when I looked at the responses to my pilot questionnaire I realised that the questions I was asking did not provide any data that was sufficiently focused on my title.' This provides a reason, so your Log now contains some evidence of reasoned decision-making.

Once you have completed a page in your Log you should *not* add to it or edit it in any way. Each review page must be dated and once the date of completion has been added, the page is complete and you should move on with your project. Before completing and dating a page, however, it is acceptable to ask your supervisor to read it. Your supervisor cannot write your Log for you but they may challenge and advise you, for example by questioning you about your level of detail or clarity.

Recording advice from your supervisor

Once your research journey is well under way, do not forget to make good use of your supervisor. Your supervisor is not a source of research information but *is* a source of critical feedback. Your supervisor will not be giving you orders to follow or giving direction to your project, but they should be providing you with both challenge and advice. When you have problems — perhaps in accessing resources that you need or in managing your project alongside other commitments — the problems will be yours to solve, but your supervisor will be a sounding board and may well have some good suggestions for you to consider. There are dedicated sections in each review page of the Log for you to record the advice that you have received from your supervisor. You do *not* have to follow any advice that your supervisor gives you, but whether you follow the advice or not your Log is the place to record both the advice given and your response to it.

 **Example**

Catherine is undertaking an EP and her working title is 'Should I become vegan? An investigation into the claimed personal and environmental benefits of a vegan diet.'

At a supervisor meeting some weeks prior to her Mid-project Review, Catherine is pleased to report that she has found so many great resources that she now has a really good understanding of the benefits of veganism. She feels ready to write up her report. She is fully convinced that everyone in the world should adopt this diet and she has already stopped eating meat. She was shocked to discover that British banknotes contain animal fat. Another strand of her research looked at cosmetics and again she was shocked to find that animals are not used just for testing but that animal products are used in the cosmetics themselves. She has looked into the carbon dioxide produced via the meat industry. She discovered that most soya beans are grown as animal feed. Catherine is delighted to share all her discoveries with her supervisor.

Advice from Catherine's supervisor included the following:

- You seem to have taken your research in a variety of directions.
- You need to be clearly focused on your chosen title.
- What aspects of 'diet' are you most interested in?
- You have mentioned things that are 'used' by human beings as well as those that are 'eaten'.
- If you are interested in environmental aspects, have you fully considered arguments that suggest eating *less* meat rather than *no* meat might be sufficient?
- Have you considered parts of the world where land is not suitable for plant agriculture?
- I suggest you choose the aspect of veganism that you have most research on and focus your title further.

- It would be better to research one small part of issues related to veganism in *depth* rather than to take a broad view looking at a wide range of issues but none in any great depth.
- I know this might seem like you have wasted some of your time but you only have 5000 words, do not waste any by drifting off-topic.

Catherine considers this advice and (slightly reluctantly) revisits her research and realises that she has lost focus. She decides not to waste the aspects of her research so far undertaken that would not be wholly relevant for her report. Instead she will refer to this slightly off-topic research in her presentation and explain why she did not include it in her report. She decides that her main focus will be on diet, as in the food and drinks consumed by human beings. Specifically, she will focus on the protein, carbohydrate and vitamin needs of a human body and analyse the ways in which a vegan might maintain full health without the consumption of animal products. She will refine her title to reflect this.

Catherine should note all of this down so that her research journey will be fully explained when she writes up her Mid-project Review.

How to use a research journal, diary or blog

You will provide evidence of the implementation and monitoring of your Project Plan in your Log, but do *not* rely on your memory alone for this. You will spend weeks or months working on your EP, and it will be hard to remember all the relevant information when you write your Log if you do not have some notes to remind you. Use some sort of research journal throughout the research and other phases of your project. You could keep rough notes, perhaps in an exercise book, or you might prefer to keep electronic notes using your mobile phone or laptop. As suggested in Chapter 1, you could set up an EP blog. It does not matter *how* you keep records of your EP activities, but do keep some kind of record or you will be entirely dependent on your memory when you come to write up your Log.

The sorts of information that you should be keeping records about include:
- **Who** you have talked to about your EP. Keep careful records of the places and times of interviews, the qualifications and titles of interviewees, etc.
- **Where** you have visited, e.g. museums, galleries, work-experience, etc. Again, times and dates should be carefully recorded.
- **Which** books, journals and articles you have read. Record carefully all the important details that will be required for your bibliography, as discussed in Chapter 6.
- All the **internet searches** you have undertaken, including those that were fruitless. Do not forget to save the complete URL of sites that might be useful, plus the date and time of access, recording all the details that will be required for your bibliography.
- Any **communication** related to your EP via letters, phone calls or e-mails. Keep original letters carefully, print out e-mails, and make careful notes during and immediately after any phone call.

> **TIP**
> Keep a notebook near your bed. Often good and creative ideas appear at unexpected times, particularly when your mind is quiet.

- Any form of **social media** material that is relevant for your EP. Screenshots should be dated, fully identified and carefully saved.
- Any **relevant** films, podcasts, TV shows or radio programmes that you have watched or listened to. The date and full details of production should be recorded.
- Any great **ideas** that you have had related to your EP — your 'eureka' moments.
- All **decisions** that you have made related to your EP.

Do not forget to write down your **thoughts** and **reflections** as your EP research develops.

This note-taking in a journal or blog does not replace your Log, but it should make your Log easier to complete. You should record details of *all* the resources you have made use of, including human beings, as you will eventually list them in your bibliography. (Bibliography and referencing will be discussed in Chapter 6.)

Making good use of your resources

Efficient reading

Most EP students will commence their research with reading. A good place to start is with a published piece of writing by an established expert in the field of study. Such writing is frequently found in secondary sources such as books and academic journals. Learning to read efficiently is an important skill to develop.

Do not feel that having selected a book for your EP you have to read it *all*. First you need to identify those sections of the book or article that are, or are not, relevant for your targeted research. There are various parts of a book that you should initially focus on:

- The contents page: This will help you identify particular chapters to focus on.
- The abstract of an article, the introduction and conclusion of a book, or the first sentences of selected chapters/sections: These may also help you identify the parts of an article or book that might be relevant for your research.

> **TIP**
> You could use mini sticky notes to identify pages or sections that your initial search has identified as possibly being relevant to your EP research, but make sure that you do not mark or damage the book's pages in any way.

Sometimes it helps to identify key words related to your EP and to seek out these words in a book or article. If a document is in electronic format this can often be achieved using the 'search' function. If a book has a detailed index, this will help you identify the pages where your key words are mentioned. If neither an index nor a search function is available, you can scan the document yourself, by eye, looking for your chosen key words.

Skim reading

Skim reading means reading something quickly to get a general idea of its meaning. It allows you to gain a 'flavour' of the content of a piece of writing before doing any close reading or note-taking. When you skim-read through an article or a chapter of a book, you do not read every word but instead you scan over the page quickly to gather a general impression of the content.

The combination of searching for relevant sections and then skim-reading those sections should help you identify the sections of written text in your various resources that require careful close reading.

Example

Using this book, especially its contents page and index, a newly appointed supervisor might identify sections, pages or paragraphs that might be relevant to 'Supervision of an Extended Project'.

A key word for them to look out for would be 'supervisor'. Every mention of 'supervisor' in this book might provide relevant information to help them learn about their new appointment. The supervisor can then skim-read the identified sections to assess their relevance.

Close reading

Close reading should be critical and take nothing at face value. It should carefully examine the arguments and evidence presented. How did the author reach their conclusions? Are you reading their opinions or is sound reasoning put forward? How were any 'facts' established to be true by the author? Have you found any different interpretations of these 'facts' in other resources? Is the author speculating about future events? What methodology has been employed? Be especially critical when looking at data. How was it collected? How does one piece of evidence compare to another? If comparing results from different experiments, how do they relate in terms of reliability?

When reading closely it is very likely that you will need to read a piece of writing more than once. Make sure that you are sitting comfortably with good lighting. If you feel your concentration slipping, take a break.

Taking notes

Much of your research will involve reading, watching and listening, together with note-taking. Learning to take notes that will be helpful when writing your EP report may take a while, but this is an important part of research. The activity of note-taking helps you concentrate and you will quickly find out if you are failing to understand something that you are reading or listening to because you will not be able to write notes about it that make sense.

A few key ideas about note-taking include:

- Write down key words and capture the significant themes and ideas.
- If much of your research comes from online resources you must resist the temptation simply to 'copy and paste' chunks of text into your notes. This will not help you absorb the information and could lead you into non-deliberate plagiarism (discussed in the next section).
- Learn the art of the *précis* (or summary). Try paraphrasing, cutting out any irrelevant information and pulling out the key snippets of relevant data and information.

- You may find that developing a form of shorthand helps you take good notes, but be sure you can understand your own shorthand. Don't worry if no one else can read and understand your notes — you are writing these for yourself.
- It is vital that you clearly label each set of notes, giving all relevant details of the resource from which they came and the date on which the notes were taken.

If taking notes at a live lecture you will need to work quickly to keep up with the speaker. It may help to use diagrams, bullet points, arrows, etc. You need to follow some form of note-taking strategy. For example, you may find it useful to follow the **Cornell note-taking system** — many students find it helps them take effective notes. The ideas included in the Cornell system also apply to notes taken from reading documents. There are many YouTube videos you can watch to find out more about the Cornell system.

When taking notes from written material, a useful skill to develop involves reading the material, covering it up and then taking notes from memory, using your own words. This will help you discover if you *really* understand what you have just read. You may find that you need to read the material several times before you feel able to take notes from memory. Similarly, if you cannot take useful notes from a recorded lecture, this probably indicates that you need to listen to the lecture again.

Some students find it helpful to use a digital whiteboard when organising their notes. Links between notes from different resources can be highlighted, so that key ideas, themes or theories can easily be identified. Other students use large pin-boards and physically link their hard-copy notes together.

There are some useful activities produced by universities available to EPQ students for a range of research skills, including effective note-taking.

> **TIP**
>
> Taking notes from recorded events is much easier than live ones in that you can pause, rewind and replay as many times as you need.

Avoiding plagiarism

Plagiarism is passing someone else's ideas or work off as your own. It is a form of theft and you should always be careful to avoid it. If plagiarism is detected in your EP it is very unlikely that you will gain any credit, meaning that you will be unlikely to receive a grade in the EPQ. It is therefore very important that you understand what plagiarism is and how to avoid it.

Referencing is a way of showing that you have used and acknowledged another person's work, ideas or opinions. Whenever you use words or ideas from one of your resources within your EP report, you should acknowledge the source. This is called 'citing' a reference or giving a 'citation'. If you fail to acknowledge the sources that you are using, you will be guilty of plagiarism. (You will find details about different ways in which you might reference your EP in Chapter 6.)

You will need to give a **citation**:
- Whenever you use a **direct quotation** from one of your resources.

Example

It is highly likely that a student writing an EP related to Martin Luther King will include some of the exact words used in King's 'I have a dream' speech. They must cite this correctly. Perhaps they have watched Martin Luther King's speech on YouTube. They should record exactly the time and date that they watched this recording and make a record of the URL, ready for use in their bibliography.

- Whenever you **paraphrase**, rewriting something that you have read or heard in your own words. Even though this is now your own writing, you are making use of ideas that are not your own and you must acknowledge the source of these ideas.

 Example

Sidrah is undertaking an EP related to artificial skin. She reads an article from the *Journal of Biomedical Engineering* entitled 'Immunological challenges associated with artificial skin grafts: Available solutions and stem cells in future design of synthetic skin'. Sidrah paraphrases the 'Background' paragraph of the article because this helps set the scene for her EP. It is very important, even though Sidrah has not copied anything out word for word, that she clearly cites the article and credits the author.

- Whenever you make specific reference to the **work or ideas** of another person you must properly acknowledge this.

 Example

The phrase 'selfish gene' is frequently used, but any ideas related to this term should not be used without giving credit to Richard Dawkins. Similarly, ideas related to the phrase 'survival of the fittest' should be credited to Charles Darwin.

ACTIVITY

Identify one key idea found in one of your resources that should be attributed to the author of the resource.

73

The only ideas that are not your own that you do *not* need to cite are those that can be deemed to be 'common knowledge', but whether a certain idea counts as common knowledge may be open to debate. If you have any doubt at all about something that you want to include in your report, it is always safest to cite a reliable source. A very common error made by students of the EPQ is to make unreferenced assertions.

 ## Example

It would be safe to write 'There are seven days in a week' without providing a reference. This is reasonable to take as 'common knowledge'.

It would *not* be safe to write 'The population of India is 1.3 billion' without clearly stating where you have taken this statistic from. The reader should be able to find out how this figure has been found in case they want to look into it further.

Examples of **potential plagiarism** include:

- Thinking that you have paraphrased when actually you have merely changed the odd word here and there. This happens very easily, particularly when the original piece of writing is eloquent and your attempt to paraphrase is clumsy in comparison. In this situation a citation does *not* excuse you from the fact that you are trying to pass off someone else's words as your own.

- Accidental or unintentional plagiarism can happen if you keep poor notes. If you fail to identify that a section of your notes is actually directly copied from a particular article, by the time you come to write your report you might truly believe that these are your own words.

- Self-plagiarism: It is not acceptable to include work in your EP that you have already completed for other purposes. For example, it is not acceptable to do an EP on the same topic as previously or currently undertaken coursework for any other qualification.

- Copying Production Log entries: It is not acceptable for you to copy another student's Log. Your Log should be unique, original and entirely yours.

- A common form of plagiarism found in EPs is the use of 'cut and pasted' sentences or paragraphs woven into the report without being identified as a quotation. Even if these are followed by a citation this still counts as plagiarism. If you use the original words of an author you *must* indicate that you are quoting them.

There are two main ways you can use somebody else's ideas when you read their writing or watch or listen to them (live or on screen):

1 If you incorporate these ideas into your EP, writing *entirely* in your own words, you must cite the source from which the ideas came. You *must* give credit — do not try to pass these ideas off as your own.

2 In some cases, you may want to reproduce *exactly* the phrasing used by the original author. In this case you must use a **quotation**. This must be *identical* to the words written or spoken and it must be clearly referenced with a citation.

ACTIVITY

Choose two of your written resources and paraphrase one paragraph from each.

How easy was it to maintain the sense of the writing but to write entirely in your own words?

TIP

The inclusion of photos, music, video clips or similar material in your EP where permission has not been sought is not acceptable. You must seek permission to use the material first and it must be clearly referenced.

Quotations up to two lines in length can be incorporated straight into the body of the text using inverted commas.

 Example

Edwards suggested that 'the cause of this abnormality is possibly due to the occurrence of high levels of iron in the soil'.

If part of a quotation is left out, this should be indicated in the quotation by the use of an ellipsis (three dots).

 Example

Dean reported that 'the use of chemical weapons … is wholly unacceptable'.

Longer quotations should be indented in a separate paragraph, with no use of inverted commas.

 Example

While writing about the Extended Project Qualification in 2019, Christine Andrews said:

> It is possible to seek out a specialist mentor as part of your research. For example, this could be an expert in your chosen field of research or someone with technical skills that you need to learn. If this is a route that you choose, keep careful records of all meetings with your mentor and provide transcripts of any interviews that take place. You should treat a mentor in the same way as a book or online article: as a source of information that requires careful critical analysis.

Carefully selecting and **copying exactly** key statements and keeping records of where they came from is worthwhile. You will probably not need to include many direct quotations in your final report, and too many quotations will interfere with the flow of your writing. But it will take you very little time to write down a few potential quotations from each resource that you use and the resulting list of possible quotations may prove to be helpful. You might introduce quotations into your report in one of the following ways:

- As Mr Smith states/believes/suggests/indicates/points out/observes/ explains/argues/outlines/contradicts/proposes/advances/ intimates, '_____'
- For example, Miss Jones has argued that '_____'
- According to Dr Yeoh, '_____'
- Anthony Andrews suggests/believes/contends that '_____'
- '_____' Prof. Stephens argues, '_____'

Remember that any quotation must be clearly referenced to its source.

Taking good notes and keeping careful records of where *all* ideas, not just the potential quotations, have come from will help you avoid unintentional plagiarism.

Using IT to keep track of your research

EP students have been known to lament in their Production Logs that they have lost all their EP work. A memory stick may have become corrupted or a laptop stolen. On occasion a school or college system may have simply 'lost' their EP work. All these examples provide evidence of just one thing: poor project management.

Learning to use IT effectively to help you as you research is important. You may receive special instruction from your school or college via your Taught Skills programme.

Resource management

You will not be required to create a reference list and bibliography until your report is complete. Learning to use free referencing software such as BibMe, EasyBib, Mendeley or Zotero from the very first day of your EPQ journey is highly recommended, however, to help you keep records of your resources. (Referencing, reference lists and bibliography are discussed in Chapter 6.)

If you prefer to use Microsoft Office to keep records of resources, visit http://support.office.com. The section on 'Add a citation and create a bibliography' explains how you can use the 'Manage sources' tab to keep a record of each and every resource that you use. Microsoft OneNote or Google Docs are two more possibilities. Whatever software you choose you will find that time spent becoming familiar with these IT research tools will be time spent well.

Folders

It would be helpful to set up dedicated folders for your research. Perhaps subdivide your research into different headings, then as you take your notes you can save them to the appropriate, **clearly labelled**, folder. Since your research phase may span several months, careful filing of your work will help ensure you don't lose any of your notes or research materials.

Some students prefer to print out their notes and have a physical EP folder with cardboard dividers. This is fine and can work well for some people, but learning to use IT to keep notes organised is a valuable skill that would be worth developing.

Backing up

Regularly back-up the devices that you are using to keep track of your research. This is absolutely essential. If you have access to an online 'cloud' for storage of documents that is independent of any particular computer, you will have solved the problem encountered by those students whose laptops are stolen or damaged. You should also consider saving your EP notes on to a back-up memory stick or external hard drive. Something as large and valuable as an EP deserves to be saved safely in several locations.

E-mailing to yourself

A very simple way to keep your work safe is to regularly e-mail relevant files to yourself. Even if your laptop is broken, stolen or simply not available, you will still be able to access your work via e-mail.

Preparing for product realisation

You should be aiming to achieve a product that is 'fully realised to a high standard' (see Appendix 5 for the AQA criteria). The term 'realised' here refers to the fact that you will create a real product. All your ideas, plans and research will culminate in the creation of either a 5000-word report or an artefact of some sort together with a shorter report. This act of creation is your product 'realisation'.

How to know when to stop researching

For any EP there is always likely to be far more potential research material available than you will have time to use. As you gather more and more research evidence you may reach a point of complete overload, unless you keep a firm hold on your plan and your stated objectives. Do not allow yourself to be side-tracked into irrelevant research. Talk to your supervisor frequently and always keep your stated aims in mind.

- For a **5000-word report** the key question is: 'Have I collected sufficient varied, reliable and relevant research evidence to allow me to form a well-judged conclusion?'
- For an **artefact product** the key question is: 'Have I collected sufficient varied, reliable and relevant research evidence to allow me to make design decisions related to my product that will be based on my research evidence?'

If the answer to your question is 'yes' then you are ready to stop researching and start working on your product.

Be very honest with yourself, however. A conclusion to a report that is largely based on your own beliefs or opinions is *not* one that can be shown to be based on research. An artefact that is designed by you according to *your* preferences and personal creativity may be of very high quality but it will not be judged highly as an EPQ artefact.

Finalising your title and aims

It is only once you have **completed** collecting your research evidence that you will be able to finalise your title and aims. It is perfectly acceptable to have a significantly different final title from the one you started with, so long as you can explain how the change has come about. In some cases, it might be that your aims changed while the title remained the same. Be aware that when judging your EP submission your supervisor will be looking for changes and/ or developments of your title, plan, aims or objectives, together with your **reasons** for these changes or developments. (See AQA criteria in Appendix 5.)

In Chapter 2 we looked at the criteria you could use to select a suitable topic for your EP, with the advice being not to worry at the beginning about the final wording of your title. At proposal stage you put forward a working title and a set of aims and objectives. Through the research phase you followed your plan, achieving many of your objectives, and making adjustments to your plan and objectives as necessary.

TIP

Avoid listing in your bibliography a large number of resources that have barely been used. An EP will usually be more successful where a smaller number of thoroughly evaluated resources have been used well and subjected to detailed critical analysis.

Now comes **decision** time. You need to formulate your final title and your final set of aims. It will be on these that your product will be judged. One question that your supervisor will be asking themselves when they come to assess your EP is 'Has this student done what they said they were going to do?'

What makes a good Extended Project title?

Successful EP titles come in many forms:

- Some students phrase their title as a hypothesis to be tested. For example:

    Hands washed with cold water alone, and not dried, will spread more bacteria than hands not washed at all.

    This is ideal for a scientific investigation. Remember that if you frame your title as a hypothesis you must be able to test it. If the hypothesis is untestable you will not be able to make a well-judged conclusion.

- Some students ask a focused question. For example:

    Was the Spitfire more instrumental than the Hurricane in winning the Battle of Britain?

Spitfires flying in the Battle of Britain

- 'Is…?'-type questions are sometimes used successfully. For example:

    Is therapeutic shoeing really necessary for horses?

    Note, however, that titles framed as questions will **not automatically be successful** as EP titles.

- 'How…?' questions usually invite description and can result in conclusions that merely summarise findings. For example:

    How do condensing boilers work?

- The exception to the above comment occurs when there are competing theories or interpretations of evidence about the topic being considered. In this case a student might reasonably compare the competing theories and, using research evidence, apply judgement to arrive at a conclusion.

Which theory or interpretation has more convincing evidence to support it? For example:

How successful has the Greater Manchester Spatial Framework been at protecting the green-belt land in Trafford?

- 'Why…?' questions can also be successful where there is no universally agreed answer and you come to a reasoned judgement, having reviewed different answers that have been suggested. For example:

  Why do female domestic violence victims sometimes stay with their abusers?

- 'To what extent…?' questions are sometimes answered well and sometimes not. Think carefully before using these words in your title. If you mention 'extent' in your title then you should be prepared to measure or judge extent. In your report you should set up criteria from which extent might be judged. In your conclusion you should provide a clear answer to the question that you have asked.
  An example of a 'To what extent…' title:

  To what extent has the chick flick genre evolved narratively and ideologically?

Other titles that are often **less successful** include:

- 'An investigation into…'
- 'An exploration of…'
- 'A discussion of…'

All three of these phrases lack focus and are unlikely to set helpful boundaries on the research question. An EP title should have a tight focus.

Other titles that are often **less successful** include:

- One-word titles, such as 'Obesity', 'Marijuana', 'Acne'.
- Titles that have more than one part to them or ask more than one question. For example: 'How and why…?'
- Titles that speculate, asking questions that cannot possibly be answered with any degree of certainty. For example:

  What materials may be used in space applications in the future?

  To what degree will the current overuse of antibiotics affect the future?

Before you fix your final title you should ask yourself:

- 'Will this title allow me to make a reasoned conclusion?'
- 'Are all terms in my title well-defined?' It is frequently the case that terms like 'society' appear in titles with no attempt by the student to clarify what they are referring to. Is this 'society' in the twenty-first century, or in any particular location?
- 'Does this title truly allow me to use the research that I have undertaken?' It is not a problem if your research has taken you a long way from your original thinking, but do not stick doggedly to your original title if your research is actually focusing on something else.
- 'Is my title grammatically correct?'

Artefact project titles

For students creating artefacts, it may be more difficult to come up with a clear, focused title. If this is the case for you, then it's even more important that in your introduction you set very clear aims.

 Example

Ayesha is creating an artefact for her EP. Her final title is: 'Creating a set of promotional posters for a client'.

The title itself brings little clarity or focus. In the introduction to her report, however, Ayesha explains that as a first step towards her EP she found herself a client and that her aims include successfully working to a brief created in collaboration with her client. Ayesha sets clear aims in terms of budget, poster dimensions, style, colour and materials. She outlines that achieving her aims means meeting all her targets in terms of budget, timings and product suitability, and her client being satisfied with the outcome. Moreover, she describes in her introduction how she has set up 'before and after' data capture using sales data that will be collected from her client to be able to judge the effectiveness of her posters in terms of promotion.

ACTIVITY

Why might the following titles *not* result in successful EPs?

- 'The economics of war'
- 'Disney princesses'
- 'The life of a TV producer'
- 'To what extent did music change between 1950 and 1990 in America and the UK?'
- 'How disability has changed in England'
- 'Has money ruined football?'
- 'How cameras developed between 2000 and 2010'
- 'Race relations in Britain since 1945'
- 'The stem cell debate'
- 'Are social media influential?'
- 'How the Chinese economy has changed in the last 70 years'
- 'The history of tartan'

Can you think of titles relating to these topics that have greater focus and *would* invite evidence-based conclusions?

Mid-project Review

The Mid-project Review with your supervisor takes place halfway through the project process. It occurs when you have completed the research phase of your project and are about to move into the production phase. Following your Mid-project Review you will commence the write-up of your report. If you have an artefact as your product you will also commence the creation of your artefact.

Your supervisor will judge the success of your EP outcome by considering the aims that you set for yourself at your Mid-project Review. In terms of your Production Log this is a critical point in your project. There should be very little change after you complete the Mid-project Review page of your Log.

By the Mid-project Review you will:
- have assembled your research
- have decided on a focused **final** title and have well-defined aims
- have set a date by which you intend to have completed your product
- have set a date for your presentation and final hand-in

At the Mid-project stage of your project you finalise your targets. Your supervisor will give you advice before you move into the 'realisation' phase of your EPQ journey. The 'planned next steps' for the realisation of your product that you describe at the end of your Mid-project Review constitute your 'finally agreed plan', as described in the AQA criteria found in Appendix 5.

Listen carefully to any advice from your supervisor, especially if they suggest that you are being over-ambitious in some of your targets. Remember that you do not have to follow your supervisor's advice, but you should record it in your Log and explain why you decide to follow it or not.

One of the hard decisions that you might have to take at Mid-project Review is deciding on which research material you will *not* go on to use. It is very hard to leave out work that might have taken many hours to collect, but this is a decision that you must make if the work will add little value or has little relevance to your final title. Don't forget to record all such decisions in your Log.

> **TIP**
>
> Do not just record what you have done in your Production Log, always provide the **reasoning behind** your decisions. **Why** have you taken this decision rather than pursuing a different option?

> **CHECKLIST**
>
> Do I understand:
> - ☐ what I should be writing in my Production Log to record my project progress?
> - ☐ how to take good notes?
> - ☐ how to file my research notes effectively?
> - ☐ what plagiarism is and how to avoid it?
> - ☐ that finalising my title and aims will require careful consideration?

6

Writing your report

LEARNING OUTCOMES

At the end of this chapter you should know:

- that EP reports are all different but should share certain key characteristics
- what to expect from your Project Product Review meeting
- how to reference your EP report
- how to create a reference list and bibliography

Writing your report

Whatever your chosen product happens to be, you will have a report to write. There is no prescribed format for an EP report. You should choose a report structure that suits the particular purpose of *your* EP. For example, for an EP with a focus on History an essay format will be appropriate. For other EPs a structured scientific report would be more suitable. To decide on the most appropriate format for your report it may help you to look up examples of academic papers that have been published on similar topics.

There are certain things that you should consider, however, whatever the nature of your EP:

- Throughout your report, keep a really tight focus on the precise wording of your title.
- Do not use a chatty style of writing — use formal language throughout.
- Give your report some form of structure.
- Fully reference any quotations and cite every source from which you have taken an idea or fact.

Avoid the use of:

- emotive language
- colloquial or slang language
- textspeak
- phrases such as 'in my opinion' or 'I believe'
- unreferenced assertions, apart from something that is considered to belong to 'common knowledge'
- stereotypical or discriminatory language

Be wary of writing sentences that are over-long or complicated. Keep sentences short and focused. The use of bullet points within an academic report is generally not recommended, but there may be circumstances where you decide that they are appropriate for your purposes.

Your report should include critical **analysis** and **application** of your research material. This will certainly include the results of close reading and careful interrogation of some written resources, and might also include analysing primary data. You should include **synthesis** between your various sources of information, meaning that you should be linking together different ideas and relating your research evidence to relevant theories, ideas and arguments. Do *not* include too many of your own ideas — it is not likely that you are an esteemed expert.

5000-word reports

One aim that you must keep firmly in mind if your product is a 5000-word report is the length of your report. If you have amassed so much research evidence that you cannot possibly cover it in depth within a 5000-word report, then you will have to take hard decisions about which strands of research you will *not* include. If your natural writing style is verbose you will need to train yourself to write concisely.

Artefact reports

If your product is an artefact, the length of the written report is not as crucial. Your report serves the purpose of underpinning your artefact. The report for an artefact project should be *at least* 1000 words long, but you do not have its length as an aim. The report for an artefact serves a purpose: it should fully communicate how each of your design decisions, related to your artefact, was taken following relevant research. It is not the number of words itself that is important. Artefact reports will often be longer than 1000 words.

 Example

Steve created a campaign to raise awareness of the threats that could affect young people when using the internet. Steve was inspired to do this by various campaigns he had experienced in the past and he obtained permission from his school to develop, pilot and deliver his campaign at his school. Steve identified initial strands that he needed to research:

- The ethical considerations in delivering materials to schoolchildren, such as parental permission.
- Campaigning: he found examples of campaigns that had been judged to be successful and those that were not successful, and in both cases the reasons why.

Once he had discovered the aspects of campaigning that were deemed to be most successful he researched the specific elements in more detail. For example:

- Posters were sometimes deemed to be successful. But what makes posters effective or ineffective? He looked at the use of colour, size, language and images.
- Lectures were sometimes found to be successful. But it seemed to depend on the popularity of the lecturer. Should he consider inviting a well-known 'personality' to deliver his message?

- Campaigns that put short films into cinemas and on to television were sometimes successful. Should he consider the creation of a short film? Did he have the skill, time and resources to do this? He certainly would not be able to put his film on at the cinema or on television, but would there be other ways he could reach his desired audience?

- Door-to-door leafleting was sometimes found to be successful. Steve considered the possibility of creating a leaflet and arranging for personal delivery to the school children he was aiming his campaign at. If such a leaflet were produced, what should it look like? How much information would be enough but not too much? Should it have images as well as words? Should it be single- or double-sided? How could he fund the production of these leaflets?

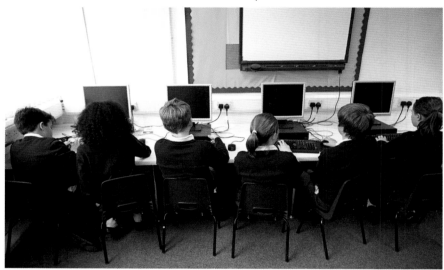

When writing the report to accompany the campaign Steve included evaluation of *all* this research to demonstrate **why** each aspect of his campaign took its particular form.

His report also included **how** he had tested the effectiveness of his campaign. This enabled him to demonstrate that he had achieved his aim. By careful use of questionnaires 'before and after' the campaign, Steve was able to show that the students who had received the campaign messages had increased awareness of the threats that could affect them when using the internet.

Report structure

Questions you might ask yourself before you decide on the most appropriate report structure for your EP include:

- How can I effectively present the outcomes and conclusions of my EP?
- Should I use charts and diagrams to display statistics in my EP? (see Appendix 3)
- Would cartoons, photographs or illustrations help convey my argument?
- Should I subdivide my report and use headings to clearly indicate each section of the report?
- Would the use of paragraphs without headings allow my argument to flow more easily?
- Should I use a report template in Word or Pages?
- Would it help to include a glossary of terms?

TIP

It is perfectly acceptable to discuss your report plan with your supervisor, but do *not* ask them to plan your report for you.

As you start to plan your report, you should decide what will be included. Some common sections that are used to structure 5000-word reports are:

- Abstract
- Introduction
- Main body
- Conclusion

Each of these sections is discussed below.

Abstract

Some EP students like to include an abstract. An abstract gives a brief summary of the contents of the report. It covers the scope, purpose, results and content of the report. It contains the 'headline' conclusion but does not get involved with the detailed analysis employed by the author. A typical EP abstract should be no more than 200 words. Longer abstracts can be found, however, such as the one in the example below, when dissertations or research reports are themselves substantially longer than an EP report.

If you decide to include an abstract, make sure it fits the description above. A good way to test your draft abstract is to ask someone who knows nothing about your EP to read the abstract. Your abstract is likely to be well-written if they can then give you a reasonable overview of what your EP is about and the conclusion it reaches.

Including an abstract is not obligatory and if you are struggling to compress your research into 5000 words it would be perfectly acceptable to include an abstract in the Summary and Reflection page of your Log.

 Example

This is the abstract of an internal research paper published in 2015 written by Ben Jones, entitled 'Does the Extended Project Qualification enhance students' GCE A-level performance?'

The skills nurtured by, and engendered through, the Extended Project Qualification (EPQ) are clearly stipulated, and have led to its becoming an increasingly popular qualification with all its stakeholders: students, colleges, employers and institutions of higher education. Future research is planned regarding the value that the EPQ adds to students' subsequent performance in higher education. The aim of this brief paper is to describe a statistical analysis of whether, and by how much, the EPQ appears to have supplementary effects on students' performance in their GCE A-levels. In other words, are the skills required by the EPQ transferable to more curriculum-embedded qualifications?

Only AQA A-level and EPQ data were used in the analyses, although permission was granted to use students' mean GCSE prior attainment scores. Since two-thirds of the national EPQ entry is currently with AQA, the results of the analyses can fairly confidently be considered to be generalisable.

Those results indicate that, after controlling for other available explanatory variables — of which mean GCSE prior attainment score is the most critical — taking the EPQ enhances the odds of achieving a higher-grade A-level (A*–B) by 29%. For each incremental grade achieved in the EPQ, the chance of being awarded a higher-grade A-level increases by 7%.

The effects were not uniform across A-level subject types, however. In most cases the impact was similar to the above figure, yet for Mathematics and Languages there was no effect.

Introduction

Every EP report needs an introduction of some kind. In the introduction you should clearly set out what the report hopes to achieve. The area under investigation should be identified, together with the goals of your research activity. Your research question should be set out, together with your selected approach for answering it. This is one place where you can provide evidence to support 'clear identification of the topic to be investigated or researched and clear evidence of appropriate aims' (see the AQA criteria in Appendix 5).

An introduction should clearly tell the reader what you have been investigating and why this topic is worthy of investigation. In your introduction you should clarify your intentions and give definitions for terms used in your title. In particular you should make clear exactly how far your research extends and clarify the scope of your project. This is equally important for artefact projects.

 Example

Bruno's EP is a short story with the title 'Follow the drinking gourd'. Bruno starts his EP with a quotation from Abraham Lincoln: 'If slavery is not wrong, nothing is wrong.' In his introduction Bruno explains that he was inspired to write a short story based on slavery following a visit to a plantation while on holiday in South Carolina. He sets out his target audience for his artefact (teenage readers). His aim is to educate young readers about slavery through fiction. He explains that the first part of his report will document the research that he undertook into both creative writing for teenagers and slavery in South Carolina. The second part of his report will show exactly how this research informed his decisions when writing the short story, including the choice of title. The final part of his report will focus on how he trialled his short story with a group of teenagers, redrafted it and trialled it with a second group, enabling him to evaluate the success of his artefact.

Main body

The structure of the main body of your EP report will be determined by the types of research you undertake.

In the main body of your report you should demonstrate:

- the use of a wide range of resources
- the ability to connect resources to your chosen topic
- the ability to analyse data
- the ability to apply findings
- an in-depth understanding and knowledge of your chosen topic
- the creation of arguments leading to a conclusion
- an understanding of the limitations of your research

You must decide whether to choose to write in continuous text using untitled sections or to subdivide the report into sections, each with its own subtitle.

If you choose to use continuous text you will interweave topic-based information throughout the main body of your report, together with argument and discussion. Themes or ideas, once identified, can extend beyond the paragraph in which they are introduced. Paragraphs will usually be linked so that your argument moves smoothly through your report. This style suits, for example, EPs with a focus on English Literature or History.

Social Science and Science reports are more likely to benefit from being divided into subtitled sections, such as Literature Review, Methodology, Findings and Discussion.

Conclusion

All EPs should have a conclusion. An EP conclusion should clearly communicate what has been achieved by the research, identifying any limitations and suggesting implications that arise from this piece of research. A conclusion might identify what needs to be done in terms of future research but you should not introduce any new material in your conclusion. Your conclusion should be based on sound judgement, having weighed up the research evidence discussed in the main body. Your conclusions, for example, should *not* be based on your personal beliefs or opinions where these are not supported by your evidence. Nor should your conclusions be based merely on a correlation. (Correlation is discussed in Appendix 3.)

For artefact projects the conclusion should relate to the artefact. Was it fit for purpose? Did it work? How do you know the answers to these questions? How was the artefact tested? Did you ask an expert in the field to judge its quality? Did you test it in some way with the intended end user or audience?

> **TIP**
>
> You should know your conclusion *before* you start to structure and write your report, but *not* before you start to research — otherwise what is the point of the research?

> **ACTIVITY**
>
> For your own EP, draw up a report plan:
>
> - How many words will you plan for the introduction and conclusion?
> - Can your research be divided up into clearly delineated subsections?
> - Which structure is appropriate?

Drafting

When you plan your report with target word counts for each section or paragraph, do not worry too much about following this precisely. What is important is that you start writing and produce a first draft, trying to include all of your relevant research material.

You should expect your first draft of your report to be too long. This is not a problem. Your first task is to complete a draft with a report structure that serves your purpose. It is a good idea to enable some form of **spell check**, ideally using British English rather than American English. The software Grammarly is particularly helpful for checking your spelling and grammar.

Once you have a first draft, the next step is editing. This may involve redrafting large parts of your report. This is perfectly acceptable and is likely to mean your report gets better each time you redraft.

Keep an eye on the word count and be ruthless in your redrafting. Be prepared to:

- cut
- rearrange content and possibly cut again
- strip out any repetition
- simplify sentences wherever possible

If you find that you are seriously over your 5000-word target, there may be sections of your report that you will need to delete altogether.

- Look carefully at the balance of content.
- Check to see if perhaps one case study has taken up too high a proportion of the report.
- Is the balance between different types of source material appropriate?
- Have you kept description firmly to a minimum and maximised the time spent on analysis?
- Have you remained fully focused on answering your title?

You may need to be selective and be prepared to remove whole sections. This can be hard to do when you have spent time carefully writing it up.

Have you used paragraphing and subsectioning effectively? Each paragraph or subsection should focus on a topic. Usually each paragraph or subsection will be making a point, one step in building your argument. Each paragraph or subsection should contain referenced research evidence to support the point being made.

In a report that uses paragraphs, each paragraph should end in such a way that it links smoothly to the next. If your report has too many short paragraphs it might be very disjointed and have no real flow. If your paragraphs are too long, however, they may be hard to read.

A helpful rough structure for your paragraphs is:

- Introductory sentence — What is this paragraph about? This might also reference the previous paragraph to ensure the report flows smoothly.
- Develop your argument — Say in more detail what the point of the paragraph is.
- Evidence your argument — What is the evidence for the point you're making?
- Analyse your argument — How does this point relate to your research question?
- Concluding sentence — Sum up the paragraph and provide a link to the following paragraph.

After editing your report to a state you are reasonably happy with, the next stage of drafting is **proofreading**. This is an essential part of the writing process. You must be **critical** of your writing style, look out for both grammatical and spelling errors, and make sure that *all* research information has been properly referenced to its source. Note that the responsibility for proofreading rests with you alone (see below for reference to the Joint Council for Qualifications regulations that govern the EPQ).

Following your proofreading you may need to do more redrafting. Each time you rewrite your revised and restructured report you should feel that you are getting closer to achieving your aims.

Project Product Review

Once you have produced a draft of your report that you are happy with it is time to hand it in to your supervisor. The Project Product Review gives your supervisor the opportunity to give you **generic** (non-specific) verbal feedback on the content and quality of your report. If you have produced an artefact, the review will also include an appraisal of the artefact. When you write up the Project Product Review page in your Log, reflect on the whole realisation phase of your EPQ journey. Evaluate the effectiveness of the plan that you finalised at Mid-project Review.

Following this review you have a final opportunity to redraft your report and make any changes to your artefact, if applicable, before handing your product in to your supervisor as complete and finished.

It is important to note at this point that *no one* should give you **specific** feedback on your report. This qualification is governed by regulations from the Joint Council for Qualifications (JCQ) and the regulations issued in September 2018 include:

> *Any explanation or interpretation given by teaching staff* must *be general and not specific to a candidate's work.*

> *Assessors* must *give details of any additional assistance on the appropriate record form.*

Parents/carers may provide their children with access to resource materials and discuss the coursework with their children. However, they must not give direct advice on what should or should not be included.

Referencing and bibliography

Referencing, as previously mentioned, is very important. It allows you to:

- acknowledge the work of other writers and researchers
- demonstrate your reading and research
- enable the readers of your report to trace your sources easily and lead them on to further information
- distinguish your ideas from the ideas that you have discovered while researching — the reader of your report should be able to distinguish your analysis from the analysis of other authors

Referencing also prevents plagiarism and helps you meet any relevant copyright regulations.

There is no preferred referencing style that you should use for your EP, but what is absolutely essential is that you learn how to insert citations into your report and how to reference your sources. There are three main styles of referencing and within those styles there are many different variations. If you move on to university you will discover that different university departments prefer different referencing styles.

Footnote style

One style of referencing is footnote style. One example of this is MHRA (Modern Humanities Research Association) and this style is frequently used in areas such as History and English. Reference information is given in footnotes at the end of each page rather than in the body of the text. If you choose to use footnotes you will list *all* the resources you have used, whether you have cited them in your report or not, in a **bibliography** at the end of your report. Footnotes should be numbered in one sequence throughout your report. When you insert a footnote, add a number in superscript in the text and create a corresponding footnote at the bottom of the page. If you use the References tab in Word, this will be done for you.

Numbered style

This form of referencing creates a numerical list of references, based on the order in which resources are cited in your report.

 Example

Freddie decides to use IEEE (Institute of Electrical and Electronics Engineers) style to reference his sources.

The following extract comes from Freddie's report:

> *The University of Southampton [1] viewed the EPQ favourably in 2018 and makes alternative, lower offers to applicants with EPQ on their UCAS form. Tim Gill [2] showed that the EPQ has a positive effect on candidate performance in their other Level 3 qualifications, such as A-levels.*

When Freddie adds the reference list at the end of his report it will look like this:

[1] University of Southampton, 'University of Southampton,' 2018. [Online] Available at: www.aqa.org.uk/subjects/projects/project-qualifications/EPQ-7993/why-choose/support-from-higher-education-institutions/university-of-southampton [Accessed 17 March 2018].

[2] T. Gill, 'An analysis of the effect of taking the EPQ on performance in other Level 3 qualifications,' Sept 2016. [Online] Available at: www.cambridgeassessment.org.uk/Images/346553-an-analysis-of-the-effect-of-taking-the-epq-on-performance-in-other-level-3-qualifications.pdf [Accessed 17 March 2018].

Note that when using a non-footnote style of referencing, you will have a reference list that refers to resources that you have cited at the end of your report but you should *also* have a bibliography that includes *all* the resources that you have used, whether you have cited them or not.

Author-date style

This referencing style is used across many disciplines. References are placed in the report itself, not in footnotes. Brackets are used for this purpose and there is an alphabetical list of references (by author name, not by order of citation) at the end of the work. APA (American Psychological Association) and MLA (Modern Languages Association) referencing includes page numbers, whereas Harvard referencing gives just the author and date of publication.

Example

Freddie decided to trial Harvard referencing instead of IEEE referencing:

The University of Southampton (University of Southampton, 2018) viewed the EPQ favourably in 2018 and makes alternative, lower offers to applicants with EPQ on their UCAS form. Tim Gill showed that the EPQ has a positive effect on candidate performance in their other Level 3 qualifications, such as A-levels (Gill, 2016).

When Freddie adds the reference list. This time it looks like:

T. Gill, 2016, 'An analysis of the effect of taking the EPQ on performance in other Level 3 qualifications'. [Online] Available at: www.cambridgeassessment.org.uk/Images/346553-an-analysis-of-the-effect-of-taking-the-epq-on-performance-in-other-level-3-qualifications.pdf [Accessed 17 March 2018].

University of Southampton, 2018, 'University of Southampton'. [Online] Available at: www.aqa.org.uk/subjects/projects/project-qualifications/EPQ-7993/why-choose/support-from-higher-education-institutions/university-of-southampton [Accessed 17 March 2018].

Note that when using a non-footnote style of referencing you will have a reference list that refers to resources that you have cited at the end of your report, but you should also have a bibliography that includes all the resources that you have used, whether you have cited them or not.

Referencing tips

Did you notice the different order and slight differences in the way the information is presented in the examples of reference lists shown above?

TIP

Remember that a reference list is *not* the same thing as a bibliography. There may be resources listed in your bibliography that are not cited in your report.

TIP

Once you have decided which form of referencing to use, stick with it.

These examples were created using the References function in Word from Microsoft Office. If you decide to use Word there will be some work for you to do, but the really hard part — getting the details expressed correctly according to your selected style of referencing — will be done for you. For each source used you must input all the relevant information and it is important that you put names of authors and other details in correctly. There are several different referencing styles from which you can choose in Word's References function, including Harvard and IEEE as shown above.

If you prefer to use free bespoke referencing software there are useful YouTube videos explaining how you can use BibMe and EasyBib to enter citations using either MLA, APA or Chicago-style referencing.

Although there is no preferred form of referencing for the EPQ and you do not have to use referencing software, the use of your own 'home-made' referencing is not recommended. For example, do not decide to insert full URLs into the body of your report.

Your school or college might teach you Harvard referencing but you may prefer to use a different style of referencing. Perhaps Chicago referencing is the style favoured by your first-choice university and you see this as a great opportunity to prepare yourself for your HE course. What is important is that you select a form of referencing that suits your EP and use it consistently throughout your report.

The use of unreferenced assertions is not acceptable in EP reports. It is good practice to write your report impersonally, for example using phrases like 'It seems reasonable to suggest that…' or 'One possible explanation is…', always making sure that you include appropriate references. Be careful not to use phrases like 'It has been argued that…' or 'The data suggests that…' without referencing such an assertion. The reader will be left asking themselves 'Who argued this way?' and 'What data is being referred to?' Sweeping statements are sometimes found within EP reports, such as 'It is widely believed that…' or 'Christians in Africa believe…', with no justification or reference to support these very bold claims.

Remember that *all* sources should be referenced, including any externally sourced images and diagrams from which you have taken information. The following is a reminder of some of the possible resource types that you might be using:

- Books
- Articles (both journalistic and scholarly)
- Web pages
- Personal communication

See Chapter 5 for examples of referencing to acknowledge the use of other people's work, ideas or opinions.

CHECKLIST

Do I understand:

☐ that I must decide how my report should be structured?

☐ that I should expect to draft and re-draft my EP report?

☐ that I should choose one referencing style and use it consistently?

☐ the difference between a reference list and a bibliography?

7

Delivering a project presentation

Specification requirements

When you start thinking about your presentation you will probably feel a mixture of things:

- **Anxiety** because you have to stand up in front of an audience and the focus will be on you.
- **Pride** because you have completed your product and it is truly all your own work.
- **Impatience** because you have been working on your EP for so long that by now you simply want to get it finished.

Good preparation will provide you with confidence. Confidence will help calm your nerves. It is worth having one final burst of energy and hard work to prepare your presentation — the end of your EPQ journey is in sight!

Let's explore what exactly an EPQ presentation should involve. Your EPQ presentation *must* be:

- delivered to your **supervisor** as part of a larger audience (minimum size of audience is two)
- **live**, you cannot deliver your presentation as a recording and there are no 'second chances' — you should treat your presentation in the same way that you treat an external examination
- supported by your answers to your supervisor's **questions**. These will be questions that you have not been specifically prepared for. You must be ready to give considered answers 'on the spot'. Questions may also be asked by other audience members, but the 'official' recording of your questions and answers is made by your supervisor in your Log, page 13, **Presentation Record Part B**

- designed for and delivered to a **non-specialist** audience. You must explain all specialist terminology and concepts carefully. You are, however, permitted to invite some topic/subject specialists to your presentation

Example

Ruben's product for his EP was a 5000-word report related to 'Écriture inclusive' and the reasons why it has caused great debate within France. During his presentation he had to carefully translate various expressions from French into English and demonstrate the issues related to the dominance of the masculine form within the French language. He invited to his presentation the teacher of French who he had interviewed as part of his research, Marie-Pierre Dupillier. She was very happy to be invited to see how Ruben's EP had developed, but the presentation was delivered carefully by Ruben, assuming no understanding of the French language by his audience.

When you start planning your presentation there may be conditions that you must abide by set out by your school or college, in addition to the exam board requirements. In many schools and colleges the date, venue, duration, audience and type of presentation will all be decided by the centre coordinator. It is important that you talk to your supervisor and clearly establish which aspects of the presentation are under your control and which aspects are decided for you by your school or college.

You should find out early on in your EPQ journey whether it will be possible for you to choose your own date and venue, and whether you will be able to invite your own chosen audience and decide yourself on the type of presentation to deliver.

What should an EPQ presentation include?

The AQA specification for the EPQ requires that each student 'prepare and give a presentation about the project product and process'. There is no detailed list in the specification dictating what should or should not be included in an EPQ presentation, however.

The content and format of your presentation should be your choice entirely, even if other aspects have been arranged and decided for you. If your supervisor gives you an exemplar presentation template to follow, you do not have to use it. Try to make your presentation unique and engaging — you should see it as an opportunity. You will be telling your audience about the fantastic experience that you have had while undertaking the EPQ. This is your chance to share the interesting discoveries that you have made, about your chosen topic area but also about yourself and your own learning. Your presentation allows you to share with your audience aspects of your EPQ journey that you might not have included in your Log or report and it gives you the chance to demonstrate the skills that you have developed.

Here are some aspects of your EPQ journey that you might like to include in your presentation, but note that none of these is obligatory:

- The topics that you initially considered for your EP, and why you settled on your actual topic.
- The planning methods that you used and why you selected these methods.

TIP

Do *not* make your presentation into a shortened version of your report. If you do, you will have wasted the opportunity offered to you.

- Resources that you found easily.
- Resources that you struggled to find.
- Resources that you chose not to use and, most importantly, why not.
- Resources that were most surprising or useful.
- Methods that you used to keep good records of your research.
- Any biased opinions that you discovered while researching.
- Methodologies that you employed, especially if you did any primary research.
- Problems that you encountered, and how you overcame them.
- How your research affected your objectives, your aims and your final title choice.
- A summary of your project product.
- How you tested and evaluated your artefact (if applicable).
- How you reached your conclusions.
- The limitations of your conclusions and how they might have been stronger.
- What you have learned about yourself while undertaking your EP — have you surprised yourself in any way?
- Where you found yourself outside your 'comfort zone' and how you handled this.
- The skills that you have developed.
- How you plan to develop this project further in the future (if applicable).
- How, if at all, this project has affected your degree/career choices.
- Advice to future students of the EPQ.

This list is by no means exhaustive nor, as mentioned above, is it obligatory. You may prefer to leave many of these aspects out of your presentation and instead write about them in your Log. If your presentation is tightly time-bound you will probably not be able to include all these aspects of your EP. You will need to think carefully about which aspects are key to telling *your* EPQ story.

ACTIVITY

Thinking about your own EP:

- Identify several key aspects of your EPQ experience that you consider important for inclusion in your presentation.
- Write each key aspect down and bullet point the parts of your research process and outcomes that are related to each of your selected key aspects.

This should give you a good presentation framework from which to start. If you cannot think of many key aspects to begin with, use the list above to help you.

Types of presentation

There is no limit to the possible forms of EP presentation.

Presentation with slides

The use of slides as a backdrop to a presentation is very common. Many students choose to present using a backdrop screen with projected slides produced using PowerPoint, Prezi, Keynote, or similar.

Do *not* treat your slides as an opportunity to write out the story of your EP, so you can read this story out to your audience. A set of presentation slides full of lines and lines of text is not conducive to an exciting and engaging presentation.

Boring slides

Do *not* treat your slides as an opportunity to write out word for word the whole story of your EP, allowing you to read this story out to your audience. There is nothing more boring for an audience than a set of presentation slides with lines and lines of text that you then proceed to read out to your audience when they are perfectly capable of reading them to themselves. This makes your presentation tedious and your audience will not be entertained, meaning concentration may start to wane and the momentum of your presentation will be lost. For the audience you will effectively be repeating yourself as they can read faster than you can speak and so those that are concentrating will have already read what you are about to say and be bored, while those that have switched off will just wait for you to speak and not bother to read the slide. This means that, instead of the slide enhancing your presentation, the slide just becomes an irrelevance. You want your slide to enhance your presentation and therefore it needs to diverge from what you are actually going to say yourself. It needs to reinforce your narrative and perhaps illustrate some of the important points you make in your presentation. This will make the presentation as a whole more interesting for your audience and increase your chances of successful delivery. A switched-on, interested audience will be more likely to appreciate all the hard work you have put into your EP. So keep your slides focused, and remember: do not fill your slides with loads and loads of text setting out everything you have prepared to say to your audience. If you do set out on your slides, word for word, everything you are going to say out loud, you run the risk of not making the most of all the hard work you have done. That would be a shame for you and for the audience who have taken the time and trouble to attend your presentation to see all the effort you have put in to your EP.

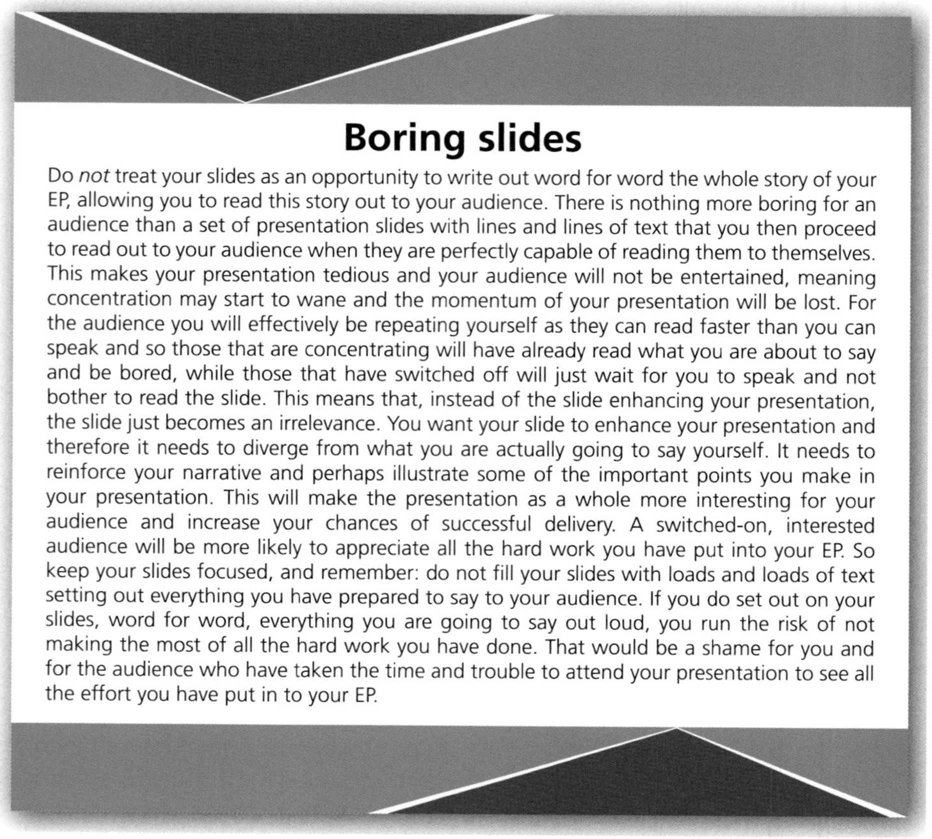

Figure 7.1 Presentation slides full of lines and lines of text do not make exciting or engaging presentations

Preparing a relevant and interesting set of slides as a backdrop to your presentation will help maintain your audience's interest. Many people have a short attention span. Your purpose in your presentation is to succinctly communicate the story of your EP. Having eye-catching slides on a screen behind you will usually make your task easier.

A good rule of thumb is to create no more than one slide per minute of planned presentation. Each slide should be visually engaging and relevant to the points you are making verbally.

Having a set of slides to project allows you to use photographs, charts and graphs to demonstrate themes discovered by your research.

The slide on page 97, top, shows a word cloud analysis of a speech made by David Cameron, the Prime Minister of the UK, just before the Brexit referendum. This was created using Wordle, which is a free online tool.

> **TIP**
>
> If you decide to use PowerPoint to deliver your presentation, have a look at the video 'Life after death by PowerPoint'. This is a humorous but insightful take on poor use of PowerPoint given by American comedian Don McMillan.

The use of word clouds can be visually very effective, particularly if you have qualitative questionnaire answers to display. The more frequently a word appears in your data, the larger it appears in the word cloud. Several websites offer free word cloud generation.

You might also decide to include some relevant video clips or photographs. You must select any animation, gifs or other visually 'busy' effects carefully, however. Too much visual stimulation might cause your audience to lose focus on your key messages.

Avoid the temptation to use a photograph or artwork as a background for your slides. The PowerPoint slide below, for instance, is not effective because the words on top of the photo are hard to read. All words should rest on a plain background, and you should ideally write words on your slides in a dark font on a light background.

Figure 7.2 Presentation slides with the words on top of a photo are hard to read

> **TIP**
>
> Using font size up to 45 for titles and font size around 24 for slide content is frequently recommended. Check all your words are clearly visible from the back of the presentation room.

Having slides allows you to leave a slide up at the end of your presentation as a backdrop, perhaps containing a powerful image or a brief summary of your EP's conclusion.

If you decide to use slides:

- Carefully check your spelling.
- Reference all the images and citations used.
- Use bullet points rather than free text wherever possible, but not too many bullets on any one slide (five is usually plenty).
- Use the same easy-to-read font for all slides (sans serif fonts, such as Arial, are best) and use the same size of font throughout.

Poster presentation

Many students present their EP findings at a 'marketplace' event arranged by their school or college. This may involve presenting alongside fellow students of the EPQ, sometimes with fifty or more students presenting their EPs simultaneously in a large hall. Very often this 'marketplace' type of event is best suited to a poster presentation.

This type of presentation is frequently used in universities. Do not think that creating a poster is an easy option, however. It will take you time to learn how to communicate effectively via a poster.

The poster that you create should communicate your whole EPQ journey. Your poster should use a sufficiently large font size for any words to be easily legible from a distance of one to two metres and have only a few key phrases written on it. Your poster should enable the reader to learn all the important aspects of your EP research and conclusions.

Viva-style presentation

Some students deliver a viva-style presentation. This means delivering to a very small audience using no presentation tools (such as slides).

It is still important to prepare carefully for your presentation if this is your chosen style. You can expect your small audience to ask you searching questions.

For some students, perhaps those suffering from anxiety, a small viva-style presentation might be preferable to preparing a presentation for a larger audience. This might also be the case if the topic of an EP is particularly sensitive or has the potential of causing distress or offence to an unprepared larger audience.

Example

Ian's EP title was 'Is the scrupulosity of some Catholics a form of OCD?' He asked his supervisor for a viva-style presentation because he did not want to offend any Catholics within a wider audience.

Tools and software

As already mentioned, there is no obligation for you to use a backdrop to your presentation. If you want to, you can simply talk to your audience. Neither do you have to create any presentation notes or cue cards. But if you reject the use of presentation software, presentation notes or a presentation poster, you must have reasons for doing so and must clearly explain these in **Presentation Record Part A** in your Log.

When selecting tools and supporting materials you should always be seeking to effectively communicate with your audience. Remember that 'communication' is included in the judgement of your EP (see Appendix 5 for the AQA criteria).

Presentation software

There are many software options for projecting slides for you to choose between, for example PowerPoint, Prezi, Keynote and Google Slides. It would be a good idea to test different options out and choose the one that suits you best. It is possible, for example, to embed information from programs such as Word and Excel into a PowerPoint presentation. Embedding video clips into a slideshow or Prezi presentation can be very effective.

Remember the well-used saying that 'a picture says a thousand words'. Using presentation software to project relevant images will help you communicate your messages.

Example

> Francis undertook an EP that investigated and evaluated different investment strategies used by UK investors. He found an article in the *Sunday Times* newspaper written by Kelly Kirby, an expert financial adviser working for a large UK firm. Francis was thrilled when Kirby agreed to be interviewed and the information from this interview was used extensively within his EP report. During the presentation Francis had a slide with the title 'My best resource'. The slide simply had a photo of Kirby, used with permission. Francis talked his audience through his preparation for the interview, the information that came from it, the triangulation he undertook to check its reliability and the use that he eventually made of the interview material.

TIP

It is risky to have embedded internet links in a set of slides unless you are *certain* that a good internet connection will be available during your presentation.

ACTIVITY

Using the list of key EPQ aspects that you identified in the previous activity:

- Create a 'snappy' title for each aspect.
- Find a suitable image to illustrate each key point.
- Using your preferred software, create a set of slides. Each slide should have a title and an image.

Tools

Cue cards are a very useful presentation tool. You may not use them at all, but just in case you feel anxious or 'lose your thread' following a distraction, holding a well-produced set of cue cards can be very reassuring. Small index cards are ideal. Use one card per slide if you are using slides, or one card per idea if you are delivering without slides. Use legible, reasonably large writing and include key points, perhaps in a bullet-point style. The cards should be clearly numbered and ideally they should be attached together by a treasury tag or ring so that the order is preserved even if you drop them. Cue cards should have *all* your key points on, noting the main ideas and concepts that you wish to mention at particular points within your presentation.

TIP

There is nothing more frustrating than reaching the end of your presentation and *then* realising that you have failed to mention something important, like a key finding of your research. It is better not to rely on your memory alone — the stress caused by having to present your findings may cause you to forget important things. It is much safer to have some written prompts.

Some students prefer to use A4-sized **presentation notes**, possibly contained in an attractive folder that can be held. If this is your preferred option, avoid the temptation to write a presentation 'speech'. It can be very effective to use one page per slide/idea and have bullet-point lists written in a very large font so that a quick glance can reassure you that you have covered everything you intended to at each stage of your presentation.

ACTIVITY

Using the set of 'snappy' title slides you created in the previous activity, for each slide write some draft notes. Include:

- Bullet points of the parts of your research process and outcome that are related to each slide.

- Amusing or memorable 'incidents' that you experienced while researching.

- Your reflections about your decisions relevant to each slide.

- Possible questions that you imagine your supervisor and/or audience might ask you based on this aspect of your EP.

Audience handouts can be very useful and give your audience an additional focus. Using handouts can also help you in your delivery to non-specialists if your EP topic is particularly complicated. You might include a glossary of terms used in your report that are of a specialist nature, or an overview map of an area under discussion, if that is appropriate. Your handout might include a brief audience questionnaire that you ask to be completed, if you are seeking some feedback.

 Example

Gregor's EP was called 'Why has the USA not gone decimal?' Gregor created a very helpful handout for his audience showing the units of measure used in the USA and comparing them to the decimal units used in Europe. He used this handout because he was aware that although the older members of his British audience would be familiar with non-decimal weights and measures, many of the younger members of the audience would be less familiar. Gregor placed a handout on each chair, so they were available to the audience as they arrived.

Think carefully about the quantity of writing on your handout, however. You do not want your audience to be distracted by reading and to not have their full attention on your spoken words. If you feel that a little background reading would help your audience to understand your EP, give the handouts out at an appropriate point during your presentation. Allow your audience a couple of minutes to read your handout.

 Example

Rajul completed an artefact EP called 'Recreating an accurate and representative WW1 trench for the set of *Journey's End*.' Rajul prepared an audience handout with a brief synopsis of the plot of the play, because he could not assume that the members of his audience were familiar with it. He handed these out following the introduction to his presentation and gave his audience time to skim-read the synopsis before carrying on.

Visual aids are always worth considering at your presentation. You could include some of the resources you used during your EP journey or the artefact(s) that you have produced. You might, for example, bring in some objects that can help explain via analogy the complexities of your research. Some students pass objects around their audience to help explain particular points. Some students use friends as models to wear certain garments or to perform certain actions.

Example

> Zainab's EP related to the use of 'financial leverage' with small and medium enterprises in China. Her report included complex mathematics related to theories used within economics. In her presentation Zainab brought in a small seesaw and used it to simplify and explain one of the theories she had been researching.

You might also use **audio aids** to enhance your presentation. You could, for example, play some relevant music as your audience arrives, or include some music or other audio at an appropriate point during your presentation.

If you decide to use presentation slides, try to obtain the use of a '**presentation remote**'. This is a device that allows you to change slides from anywhere in the room so that you do not feel anchored to your laptop. If you cannot obtain a presentation remote then ask a friend to change the slides for you and have an agreed signal that indicates 'please change slide now'. Alternatively, you could choose to use presentation software like Keynote Remote if you are using iOS devices. This enables you to control your slideshow from your iPhone or iPad.

Planning your presentation

You are required to prepare your presentation and to provide evidence of your planning in your Log, page 12, **Presentation Record Part A**. Make good use of this page, as it allows you to demonstrate more of your planning and monitoring skills.

When you start planning your presentation, think of presentations that you have attended yourself:

- When have you been bored by a presentation? What was it about the presentation that failed to keep your attention?
- When have you felt inspired by a presentation? What did the presenter do to inspire you?

Your aim is to capture your audience's attention, then keep them fully engaged and interested.

As mentioned earlier, you must establish if there are any school or college guidelines that you need to follow. For example, do you have an imposed time limit? If you do, you must carefully consider the timing of your presentation — but even if no limit is set, you do not want to bore your audience by delivering a long, rambling presentation. Most students find they can successfully communicate their EP experiences in a presentation that lasts between ten and fifteen minutes.

Start your presentation with a suitable attention-grabber. For example:

- a controversial quotation
- a question for the audience to involve them from the outset
- a 'shocking' statistic
- something very current in the news

TIP

Do not forget to explain *all* your decisions about your presentation in your Log.

TIP

Editing your EP presentation and cutting out boring or irrelevant sections is just as important as editing your EP report.

Example

Dan's EP involved an evaluation of two different treatments offered to patients suffering from macular degeneration. At the start of his presentation Dan included slides to demonstrate to his audience how this condition affects the sight of patients. The view from Dan's bedroom was shown on screen as seen by someone with normal vision and then shown again as seen by someone with varying degrees of damage to the eye. Dan had included research that enabled him to create these slides as part of his EP.

The right image shows the effects of severe macular degeneration

Usually it is sensible to have the same title for your presentation as for your EP report. Sometimes, however, you might have a good reason to call your presentation something different. In such a case you should refer to your final EP title at some appropriate point during the presentation.

Your presentation will require a structure that allows your audience to follow it with ease. It is your choice, however, how it should be structured. In the same way that your report structure is yours to decide, so is the structure of your presentation. You will need some form of introduction, main body and conclusion.

You might include some of the following:

- A brief sketch of your report, similar to an abstract (see Chapter 6).
- Examples of resources that you selected to use and/or examples of resources that you rejected.
- Selected methodologies, including for your project management, with reasons for their choice.
- Decisions that you made during your EP journey.
- Evaluation of your project as a whole and/or evaluation of your own learning.
- Audience participation — you could, for example, plan to ask some questions at appropriate points.

TIP

It is probably best *not* to write a script for your presentation or try to learn it as though you were performing a play. Do not try to memorise your speech, but to calm your nerves you could memorise the introduction to your presentation.

TIP

In exactly the same way that you do not want your EP report to just be a narration or description, you should be aiming to fill your presentation with reflection and evaluation (see Chapter 8).

103

Example

Siobhan's EP related to the changing fauna and flora of her local canal. For her presentation Siobhan took her audience on a guided walk along the canal.

It is a good idea to end your presentation with an effective conclusion that leaves your audience with a good final impression. If you can find one, plan to finish with an appropriate punchline so that the audience is left with a sense of completion.

Use of humour in your presentation is great so long as the humour is non-offensive and not forced. Think carefully, however, before planning to include humour in your presentation. A joke that falls flat may knock your confidence. The use of cartoons or Clipart within presentation slides can be an effective source of humour.

The type of presentation, venue and audience will clearly affect your planning. For example, some students:

- present during timetabled time, using on-site equipment in their usual EPQ base and their fellow EPQ students as their audience
- invite a selected audience and present during a lunch hour, or at the end of the school/college day, having themselves booked an appropriate location and arranged for the appropriate equipment (e.g. laptop, screen and projector) to be present
- prefer to deliver their presentation using a less formal seminar layout with the audience and the presenter all seated in a circle
- are very creative with their presentations, and take this as an opportunity to develop and demonstrate new skills
- use the presentation as an opportunity to gather feedback on their product and ask the audience to complete some form of evaluation

TIP

In your planning do not forget to include a thank-you to your audience for their attention at the end of your presentation.

Example

Luke created, as an artefact, a set of desserts with very low sugar content, designed for people with type 2 diabetes. At his presentation he invited his audience to a 'blind tasting' using some of his desserts and also some commercially available diabetes-friendly desserts. He was looking for honest evaluation of his product from as wide a range of tasters as possible. Luke had already received feedback from some volunteers with type 2 diabetes, but he saw the presentation as a great opportunity to gather more data. This data would not contribute to his finished report, but he would be able to reflect on it when writing his **Summary and Reflection** page in his Log.

Very particular planning is required for some students, for example if they have sensory impairment of some kind.

Example

Frieda has severe loss of hearing and uses British Sign Language as her primary form of non-written communication. As part of her presentation planning Frieda organised an interpreter so she could sign her presentation and have her interpreter deliver it verbally to the audience.

Practice makes perfect

If you want to wow your audience it is absolutely vital that you build in plenty of practice time.

Practising your presentation can begin months before your presentation is scheduled. Your supervisor might offer you practice opportunities:

- Sometimes students are invited to deliver a Dragons' Den-style presentation at proposal stage.
- Sometimes students are invited to present their EP 'progress so far' mid-way through the process.

It can be really helpful to take up these opportunities, if they are offered. Ask your supervisor and fellow EPQ classmates to give you some feedback. Constructive criticism is what you are looking for so that you can improve your presentation style and delivery.

TIP

You can use and reflect on any information gathered from feedback following your practice presentations in both the **Presentation Record Part A** and the **Summary and Reflection** section of your Log.

ACTIVITY

Arrange a practice presentation of 'My EPQ journey to date' and find an interested audience. You could ask your family or friends if there is no opportunity to deliver to your EPQ classmates or supervisor.

At the end of your presentation ask your audience to fire questions at you. These will not be the questions that you will eventually answer 'on the day', but they should help you build up confidence in facing unprepared questions.

Give each member of the audience an evaluation sheet like the one below and ask them to complete it as fully and honestly as they can. At the end of the presentation gather the sheets in and use your feedback to identify ways in which you can improve your presentation skills.

Presentation evaluation sheet

Aspect	Comments
Venue well prepared?	
Started and ran to time?	
Presenter speech clear and audible?	
Pace of presentation	
Body language	
Use of humour	
Effective eye contact?	
Use of notes / cue cards	
Quality of visual presentation used (PPT/Prezi/etc.)	
Effectiveness of any props or aids used	
Any handouts? Did they add to presentation?	
Was the presentation well-prepared?	
Did the presenter stay focused?	
Good overall understanding of EP topic shown?	
Questions answered well?	
Strong summary / powerful conclusion?	
Overall were the audience engaged?	
General overview of performance	

Figure 7.3 An example of a presentation evaluation sheet

Another exercise that you might try is 'blindfold' communication. Try to communicate to a friend using words only. How much do you need to use your hands or facial expressions? How many clues do we derive from the body language of a presenter when we are sitting in an audience?

ACTIVITY

Try presenting to yourself using a mirror, or set up a camera and film yourself as you practise delivering your presentation.

Be especially critical of your use of body language and answer the following questions:

- Were you fiddling with your clothing or hair while speaking?
- Did you look excited about your research?
- Were you continually looking at your audience?
- Was your voice loud, clear and delivered at a suitable pace?
- Was the timing of your presentation right?

You should identify areas that require improvement and/or practice.

Think about what makes a good public speaker

TIP

There are many YouTube videos focusing on filler words that may help you recognise issues with your own use of such words.

When practising your presentation you might discover that you use verbal 'fillers' or slang language. The use of slang or of fillers (e.g. 'you know', 'okay?', 'um', 'err', 'like', 'basically') is something that you should train yourself to resist. This will make your presentation more professional.

Changing the pace of your delivery at appropriate points can help keep your audience engaged. A varied pace is something to aim for — speak fast to excite your audience, speak slowly to emphasise your key points. Don't be frightened by pauses in your delivery. Pauses can be used to add emphasis. Pausing before answering a question can help you gather your thoughts.

The more that you prepare for and practise your presentation, the more easily you will be able to deliver it and the more confident you will become. Confidence will help deal with the inevitable nerves that you will experience on the day of the 'real' live presentation.

 Example

> Zaidirah was worried about her use of English within her presentation, in particular about public speaking in her second language. Zaidirah rehearsed her presentation with her teacher of English and acknowledged this in her Log.

Encourage your family and friends to ask you lots of questions about your EP. If you find any that you cannot answer, consider why this is. Is it because you have already forgotten key aspects of your topic, or was the question outside your area of research? You should take time to read and re-read your EP report so that you are very familiar with it prior to your presentation.

Once you feel that you have got your presentation to a good standard, ask your supervisor to watch you present. Then listen carefully to any advice or suggestions and fine-tune the plans, slides, handouts, etc., so that you have an excellent presentation all ready to be delivered.

You should record *all* advice received, and how you responded to it, in **Presentation Record Part A**, page 12 of your Log.

On the day

Dress appropriately but comfortably, including footwear. Unless the nature of your EP means that some form of extravagant or fancy dress is appropriate, it would usually be sensible to dress smartly. Presentation clothing should be similar to the clothes you would wear to an interview.

 Example

> Jiang was presenting her EP. Her artefact was a costume designed for a local production of *Tales from Tolkien*. Her costume was for an Ent (a walking tree-like creature). Jiang was not in the room as her audience assembled but at the appointed time she slowly walked in wearing her costume, with an extract of music from the production playing. This made a very stunning and attention-grabbing start to her presentation. Once in the room, however, Jiang slipped out of the costume and transformed into a well-dressed and professional-looking sixth-former.

Here are some simple steps to take that should help your presentation go well:

- Arrive in good time.
- Check that all audio-visual equipment is working.
- Check there is a visible wall clock that you can see easily. You do not want to be forever glancing at your watch or phone to check the time.
- If using a screen, check that it is clearly visible to all members of the audience.
- Think about where you will stand, making sure you will not be blocking the audience's view of the screen.
- Arrange the furniture to suit your purposes.
- Do not overdo your consumption of coffee or energy drinks as your nerves build up. It is much better and safer to sip water.

TIP

It is acceptable to receive advice from others to help you improve your presentation. Your supervisor is a great source of advice but you can also ask your family and friends for help.

TIP

What will you do if the technology fails to work? Have a plan B ready. Do not rely on one memory stick, bring a back-up and e-mail your presentation notes, slides, etc., to yourself.

TIP

If you make a mistake in your presentation, simply correct the error and carry on.

- Have a bottle or glass of water within easy reach in case you need it.
- Relax while waiting for your audience to arrive. Try deep breathing: inhale deeply and then exhale completely.
- Make sure that your phone is turned off.
- Smile — this will make you feel better.

At the beginning of your presentation:

- Welcome your audience and check that everyone can hear you, including audience members seated right at the back of the room.
- If necessary, invite members of the audience to move closer to the front.
- Explain at the start how you intend to structure the presentation.
- Give an idea of your anticipated timings and explain whether you intend to take all questions at the end or whether you will give the audience more than one opportunity to ask questions.
- Politely ask your audience to turn off their phones.

If you are standing while presenting don't stand rigidly stock still — move around the room in a relaxed fashion instead. Avoid standing with your hands on your hips or in your pockets. Also avoid perching casually on a table, standing with your arms folded across your chest or with your arms behind your back. It might help you to hold something in your hand, such as a presentation remote, a whiteboard marker pen, your cue cards or your presentation notes folder.

The most effective presentations are those where the speaker has an impromptu style of speaking — the more spontaneous your presentation appears to be, the better. Try to keep a sparkle in your voice, to project your excitement and enthusiasm for your EP. Present with energy, animation, confidence and conviction. Remember to look at your audience, do *not* keep glancing at the screen (if you are using one).

ACTIVITY

Complete the following table a couple of hours before your presentation.

Action	Tick when completed	Date
Do you have your presentation slides (if applicable) with you and saved in at least two places?		
Have you checked out the presentation venue? Have you tested the projector, speakers (if required) and screen?		
Is there a visible clock in the room? If not, have you got one ready to take with you?		
Do you have a bottle of water ready to take with you?		
Have you checked that you can be heard at the back of the room? If you cannot be heard, have you arranged for a microphone to be set up?		
Have you practised a full run-through at least twice?		
Have you read through your EP report recently? Does it all still make sense to you?		
Have you made a set of cue cards/presentation notes and firmly attached them together?		
Is your mobile phone switched off and put out of temptation's reach?		
Are your presentation props/handouts safely stored and ready to use?		
Are you ready to face questions about any aspect of your EP?		
Are you ready? This is your day: you are the expert, this is your unique and individual EP. Are you smiling?		

The question and answer session

At the end of your presentation your supervisor will manage a question and answer session, the Q&A. This serves an important purpose and you should have prepared thoroughly for it.

The Q&A allows deep and searching questions to be asked about your topic area. The Q&A also provides an opportunity to demonstrate the skills that you have developed. Questions might be asked related to any aspect of your EP, not just about the contents of your report.

Example questions:

- How did you become interested in feline obesity?
- Why did you build the model using cardboard?
- I noticed several Wikipedia references in your bibliography. Can you talk us through why you included them?
- What was it about Enid Blyton's writing that surprised you most?
- How did you test your recycled gym equipment?
- Can you please explain the steps you took to ensure that your primary research at the day centre was ethically acceptable?
- Would you mind taking us through the importance of prime numbers to cryptography again?

Questions should not be generic, they should be directed at *you* and relating specifically to your EP. You should take every question as a compliment. You have interested your audience and they want to know more about your EPQ experience.

ACTIVITY

Read through your presentation and write one question relating to each section/slide. Try to put yourself in the position of your audience:

- What might they find intriguing?
- What might they want to know more about?

Some things to consider when facing questions:

- Sometimes it might help you to paraphrase the question and then ask the questioner 'Have I understood you correctly?' before answering the question. This helps clarify the question and also gives you some 'thinking' time before answering.
- Address your answers to the whole audience, not just to the questioner. You need to keep the whole audience engaged.
- Do not be afraid to admit it if you cannot answer a question. It is much better to be honest. Try to explain why you do not have the required knowledge, or perhaps suggest how you might one day be able to answer the question. Some audience members become very excited by an EP topic and they may ask questions that refer to issues outside the narrow focus of your EP. You should politely explain that your research was not looking in this direction.

TIP

Be prepared to answer questions asked by your supervisor and audience.

Presentations from members of groups

Group projects can achieve outcomes that are much greater than those achieved by an individual student. As mentioned in Chapter 1, however, each member of a group will be assessed separately on their individual research journey and on their individual contribution to the resulting artefact.

The presentations from individual members should be entirely separate. The presentation offers each member of a group a great opportunity to demonstrate exactly what they individually contributed to the group project.

 ## Example

Bilal, Josh, Kieran and Manisha worked together to collect data related to traffic movements and behaviour in the small, frequently congested town in which they live.

Bilal focused his research on the most appropriate statistical methods to employ in order to persuasively interpret the data that would be collected. Having undertaken secondary research, he analysed the raw data collected by other group members using the statistical methods he had identified as being most appropriate. Bilal also analysed public health data related to conditions connected to air quality.

Josh focused his attention on air quality. His secondary research included reading reports relating to diesel emissions and the rise in asthma-related illnesses. He was able to use equipment on loan from his local university. He undertook primary data collection and analysis. He analysed air samples taken at different locations in the town at different times. He used a monitoring device that detected nitric oxide (NO), nitrogen dioxide (NO_2) and sulphur dioxide (SO_2). He passed his raw data on to Bilal.

Kieran was interested in journey times and in comparing modes of transport used to move from one side of town to the other. His research included looking into the history of public transport in the town. He collected primary data that investigated the number of people using each vehicle that passed chosen points in the town. To do this he had to get permission to undertake traffic counts from the Highways Department. Kieran also passed his raw data to Bilal.

Manisha's focus was on campaigning. She had the task of putting the different strands of work together. The group having collected data and statistically analysed it, she decided what to look at next. Manisha researched political activism. How had people with a grievance made themselves heard in the past? It was Manisha's task to find out how their concerns about the impact of traffic congestion on the health of the town's inhabitants could be communicated to those with the power to do something about it.

Once they had collected and analysed the data, the group presented their findings to County Hall. Their campaign was instrumental in releasing funding for a road-widening scheme and the creation of designated cycle paths.

The four students created EPQ presentations that were entirely different:
- Bilal delivered a presentation using Prezi.
- Josh set up a video camera when he was monitoring the air quality, and within his PowerPoint presentation he included a video extract that showed how he went about his primary data collection.
- Kieran also used slides but he preferred to use Keynote on his laptop.

- Manisha used lots of audience participation in her presentation, taking her audience along her own journey of discovery related to political campaigning. She arrived at her presentation riding a bicycle.

Note there is no requirement that presentations from group members should be delivered on the same day. Each group member is treated separately, with their own unique Q&A session.

How does your presentation relate to the judgement of your EP, made by your supervisor?

Judgement of your EP is undertaken by your supervisor on the basis of **evidence** submitted by you. Your supervisor will consider evidence from your Log, your product and your presentation. All three of these contribute to the judgement that will be made, largely based on your demonstration of skill development (see Appendix 5 for the AQA criteria).

To give just a few ways in which your presentation contributes to this judgement:

- A carefully **planned** presentation provides evidence that supports criteria in the first section (AO1).
- Research into, evaluation of and use of **appropriate software** provides evidence that supports criteria in the second section (AO2).
- In your presentation you can explain and clarify your **decision-making**, thus providing evidence to support criteria in the third section (AO3).
- In your presentation you can also demonstrate how you reached well-judged and evidence-based **conclusions**, together with evaluation and reflection of your EPQ experience, which provides evidence to support criteria in the fourth section (AO4).

CHECKLIST

Do I understand:

☐ that I have just one opportunity to present my EP findings to an audience?

☐ that the use of presentation tools and software is optional?

☐ that it is for me to decide how my presentation should be structured?

☐ that I should carefully plan and practise my presentation?

☐ that I should document my planning and practice for my presentation in my Log?

☐ that the question and answer session allows me to show just how far my research has taken me?

8 Reviewing your project

Reflection and evaluation

The development of your ability to think and write in an evaluative way, taking an objective view of both your project and of your own learning, is important. The quality of your reflection will be judged by your supervisor (see Appendix 5 for the AQA criteria).

In your Log you should explain why you have made choices/decisions and discuss any problems that you have encountered. This provides evidence of your reflection throughout your project journey as you continually evaluate your progress.

During your presentation you may choose to include reflection and evaluation, thus providing more evidence of these two required aspects:

- Evaluation of your EP
- Evaluation of your learning and performance

The **Summary and Reflection** page of your Log (page 14) gives you one last chance to evaluate the success of your completed EP, including your performance at your presentation. You are invited to reflect on the strengths and weaknesses of your completed project *and* on the strengths and weaknesses of your own learning during the project process.

Think carefully about what you have discovered while undertaking the **project**. For example:

- What did you enjoy?
- What did you dislike?
- What did you find most challenging?
- What new expertise, skills and knowledge have you gained?
- What skills that you already possessed have you improved?
- How difficult did you find it to plan and complete your work independently?
- What was successful? How have you judged success?
- Have you fulfilled your original aims and objectives?
- Would you do anything differently if you were to start again?

- Did you choose to use any tools or skills that you would not use again? If so, why would you choose not to use them in the future?
- Did things go wrong during your project journey? If so, how did you overcome the difficulties encountered?
- Did you make any mistakes? If so, were you able to rectify them?
- Are you pleased with your project outcome? If not, why not?
- Were there any resources that you did not check out thoroughly and had to abandon?
- Did you experience any dips in motivation? What were they? Why do you think they occurred?
- Do you plan to develop your project further in the future? If not, why not?
- What is the most important/useful skill that you will take away to use in the future? For example:
  - Referencing
  - Project management
  - Interview skills
  - IT skills
  - Time management
  - Presentation skills
  - Personal organisation
  - Determination/resilience
  - Independence
  - Something very personal and unique to you

Think about your **presentation** and answer some of the following questions:

- Was it successful? How do you know?
- Did you get your messages across to your audience?
- Did you stick to the planned timings?
- Were your handouts or props well received?
- Did all your audio-visual equipment work?
- Did your planning result in a presentation to be proud of?
- Did you manage to maintain eye contact with your audience?
- Did you receive a round of applause? Was this just polite or really enthusiastic?
- How well did you answer questions? Did you stumble over any?
- Did you collect any useful feedback relating to your project outcome?
- Were you pleased with your delivery and performance?

Do not gloss over any mistakes or disappointments. Nobody is perfect. Even with excellent planning you may experience disappointments or make mistakes. The important thing is that your Log accurately reflects such experiences and explains how you dealt with them. Your task is to celebrate the strengths of your EP but also to acknowledge the weaknesses. By recognising areas that could have been better you demonstrate understanding and offer the possibility of improvement for the future.

TIP

When reflecting on your EP in your Log, you need to be **succinct**. Try not to repeat things that you have already included elsewhere. Do not write a four-page detailed and rambling 'stream of consciousness'. Your Log, like your report, needs consistent relevance and focus. Concision and direct communication are required — aim for quality, not quantity.

 Example

Mia undertook an EP called 'Pieces of eight', which involved investigating this ancient form of money. She created a lesson (as an artefact) about this topic aimed at Year 6 students. In her **Summary and Reflection** page Mia communicated with great enthusiasm how her ambition is to become a primary school teacher. She was clearly thrilled by all the observations she undertook at her local primary school. She had learned a great deal about how to teach Year 6 children. Mia also explained how surprised she was when undertaking her research. She had expected to remain in the world of pirates, treasure and shipwrecks. Her EP inspiration came from Long John Silver's famous parrot in *Treasure Island*. Her research journey, however, led her to understand that 'pieces of eight' could be considered the first global currency. She was very interested to discover that pieces of eight were legal tender in the USA until 1857.

'Pieces of eight' or the 'Spanish dollar' — the world's first global currency

Every comment made in Mia's **Summary and Reflection** page referred directly to her own unique experiences. For example:

- At her presentation she arrived dressed as a pirate with a toy parrot on her shoulder. Mia reflected soberly on the wisdom of wearing an eye patch and subsequently tripping over her laptop cable, perhaps due to her restricted vision.

- Mia had problems with a pair of 'naughty' girls in the Year 6 class during the delivery of her lesson and she had to ask the class teacher to intervene.

Mia did not gloss over the problems that she experienced but showed how she had learned from them.

It can be hard to step back and assess your own strengths and weaknesses. Here are a few areas to consider:

- Did independent working suit you? If not, why not?
- How did you cope without a teacher setting you deadlines? Did you stick to your own schedule?
- Were you well-organised or were you disorganised?
- What about your 'people' skills? Did you succeed in your personal contact with other people, even if it was only your supervisor?
- Did you procrastinate? If so, how did you overcome this?

Create tables like the ones shown below to analyse your strengths and weaknesses, and fill in as many cells as you can. Don't worry if you cannot find an aspect of your project or learning to go in every cell. Only make specific comments that relate to your EP.

Table 8.1 Analysis of strengths and weaknesses — project

Aspect of EP	Strengths	Weaknesses
Choice of topic		
Planning		
Monitoring		
Selection of resources		
Evaluation of resources		
Use made of resources		
Note-taking		
Report structure		
Introduction		
Conclusion		
Referencing		
Presentation		
Anything else you might want to consider		

Table 8.2 Analysis of strengths and weaknesses — personal

Aspect of my own development	Strengths	Weaknesses
Confidence		
IT skills		
Public speaking		
Academic writing		
Communication		
Time management		
Resilience		
Knowledge		
'People' skills		

Everything that you write in your Reflection should be completely personal to your project. Sweeping, generic statements are a waste of time unless they are supported by evidence from your own project experiences.

 Example

Timo's **Summary and Reflection** page included the following:

I have learned so much by doing my project. I have learned how to manage my time and use Harvard referencing.

When Timo's report is read, however, it is discovered that he has used footnotes and has *not* used Harvard referencing. Within his Log, no evidence is found to suggest good time management. Timo had originally intended to enter for the November series of the EPQ, but his lack of effective time management resulted in submission for the following series in May. The reader of his **Summary and Reflection** page is left with a strong impression that Timo took his ideas from elsewhere, because there is a serious mismatch with the evidence found in his EP submission.

Artefact projects

Students with artefacts as their products should include evaluation of their completed product within their report. Within their planning they will include a means by which their artefact might be evaluated. For some artefacts it will be best to ask the intended user or audience for feedback after 'testing' the artefact. For other artefacts it might be appropriate to ask an appropriate expert to judge the artefact to decide if the intended aim has been achieved. In other cases it will be more a question of the student asking themselves, 'Does my artefact "work"?'

 Examples

For his EP Gus created a picture book for preschool children, with the aim of introducing the idea of reducing plastic waste. Gus understood that he would not be able to work directly with the children. Gus contacted three different nurseries and two of them agreed to use the book during 'story time' with the children. Gus also put a notice in his local parish magazine asking for 'volunteer' parents who would be willing to read the book with their preschool children. Gus designed and piloted a questionnaire to be completed by the adults who had agreed to 'test' his book and with it he collected valuable feedback on how the children had responded to his book. Gus was thus able to evaluate his book, using evidence from users, and to discover to what extent he had succeeded in his aims.

For his EP Peng sought out a client and worked to a brief from this client. Peng designed a new website for his client's business. As part of Peng's evaluation he included his client's assessment of the outcome and of whether all the requirements of the brief had been fully met. Ultimately the fitness for purpose of Peng's website could only be appropriately judged by the client.

In the conclusion to a report that accompanies an artefact, you need to judge whether your artefact achieved its intended purpose. This judgement can only be made on the strength of evidence, with the type of evidence dependent on the nature of the artefact (see Chapter 6).

 Examples

Ellie designed and built an underwater timing device that could be used by members of a synchronised swimming team. The evaluation of this device was based on evidence that:

● it was waterproof
● it kept perfect time
● it was clearly visible to the swimmers while underwater
● the team's timings improved and they were better synchronised when using the device

Maria created a piece of 'street art' for her EP and, having gained appropriate permissions, she designed and then painted a wall of a building in her home town. Maria had researched many different street and graffiti artists and she secured agreement from two such artists that they would come to give their professional opinions on her completed artefact. In addition to this, Maria used social media to collect opinions from members of her local community to discover if the message of her artwork was being successfully delivered.

Group projects

Group projects offer lots of potential evaluation. Each individual group member can consider questions such as:

- How did the group dynamics work?
- Was each member of the group fully engaged?
- Did we experience any group disagreements? If so, how were these resolved?
- Would I choose to work as a member of a group again?

Example

Holly worked with just one other person, Pete, on a group EP with an artefact product. The product was a go-kart that they would enter into a local competition. Holly was the driver of the go-kart and her research included finding the best clothing and protective gear for her to wear within fixed budget constraints.

In her **Summary and Reflection** page she discussed the problems encountered between her and Pete. For example, she would have liked to spend the Easter holidays doing some serious test drives but Pete had a two-week family holiday booked. Another frustration that arose was down to poor communication between them, so that they failed to fully communicate component costs to each other and ended up over-budget. Overall the paired-working was successful, however, and their go-kart took second place in the competition. Holly found much to write about in her Reflection, as working in a group had taught her many things.

TIP

Try to evaluate your project progress throughout your Log — do not save it all until the **Summary and Reflection** page.

CHECKLIST

Do I understand:

☐ that I should be evaluating both the project as a whole *and* my own learning?

☐ that I should make good use of the opportunity offered by the **Summary and Reflection** page of the Log to evaluate my EP in an objective way?

☐ that the **Summary and Reflection** page in my Log should accurately reflect my unique personal experience and should not contain generic summative comments?

☐ that I should include evaluation of my product within my report, if my EP product is an artefact?

9   Submitting your work

LEARNING OUTCOMES

At the end of this chapter you should know:

- which documents *must* be included in your EP submission
- what additional materials *might* be included in your EP submission
- what additional materials should *not* be included in your EP submission
- that the way you compose your EP submission is up to you

You have finished! Your product is completed, your presentation has taken place and you have carefully reflected on your EP experience. It is time to put your final EP submission together, ready to hand in to your supervisor.

There are two essential items that must be submitted:

- A completed Production Log, including signed acknowledgement from your supervisor that your presentation took place.
- Your project product, either a 5000-word report or an artefact of some kind together with a shorter report (minimum 1000 words).

Your Production Log

Throughout this book you have received advice about the completion of your Log. Your Log should be concise and evaluative. It describes your complete EP journey from the initial thoughts you had when choosing a topic right up to your reflections on the completed project journey.

The front cover of the Log (page 1) is your **Candidate Record Form**. Read each section of this front page carefully as you complete it and sign it. When you sign the Candidate Record Form you are confirming that your EP has been produced by you alone, that there is no plagiarism and that no one has written any part of your report for you. If you produced an artefact, you are confirming that no one helped you create your artefact who has not been acknowledged. If anyone has helped you with your EP and is *not* clearly acknowledged either in your Log or in your product, you must declare this help and give details. If you have used any resources that are not acknowledged, either in your Log or your product, you must declare them and give details.

When you hand in your completed Production Log the following pages will be incomplete:

- Page 2 (Submission Checklist)
- Page 3 (Taught Skills Element)
- Page 4 (Record of Marks)

Your supervisor will sign the Candidate Record Form (page 1), confirming that the submitted project is all your own unaided work, then they will complete the **Submission Checklist** (page 2), the **Taught Skills Element** (page 3) and the **Record of Marks** (page 4) *after* you have handed in your full EP submission.

For the rest of the Production Log:

- You will have completed and dated page 5, **Record of Initial Ideas**, just prior to submission of your Proposal (see Chapter 2).
- You will have completed, signed and dated page 6, **Part A: Candidate Proposal** (see Chapter 2).
- Your supervisor will have completed, signed and dated page 7, **Part B: Supervisor's Comments on Candidate Proposal** (see Chapter 2).
- Your Coordinator will have completed, signed and dated page 8, **Part C: Centre Coordinator's Approval of Candidate Proposal** (see Chapter 2).
- You will have completed and dated page 9, **Planning Review** (see Chapter 3).
- You will have completed and dated page 10, **Mid-project Review** (see Chapter 5).
- You will have completed and dated page 11, **Project Product Review** (see Chapter 6).
- You will have completed and dated page 12, **Presentation Record Part A** (see Chapter 7).
- Your supervisor will have completed, signed and dated page 13, **Presentation Record Part B** (see Chapter 7).
- You will have completed page 14, **Summary and Reflection** (see Chapter 8).

Note that that you will already have dated each section of the Log at the relevant time and you must not edit any page of your Log after it has been dated.

Check that all pages of your Log are printed out correctly and fasten the pages together with either a staple or a treasury tag. Check that every page has your **candidate number and full name** at the top.

Example

Jake reached the end of his EP and read through his Log. He realised that when he set out on his EP, ten months ago, he had few evaluative or planning skills and that this was clearly evident in his Log. Jake was tempted to over-write his Log to make it look 'better'. Luckily for Jake he mentioned this to his friend Gemma, who explained that this was not allowed.

Gemma understood that the EPQ is all about development of skills. She explained to Jake that it was important for the reader to see, by means of an *honest* Log, that Jake's planning skills had improved with time and that the depth of his evaluation had increased.

Your Extended Project report

You must decide how to present your project report. Have you:

- Chosen a sensible font and font size so that your report is easy to read?
- Used appropriate formatting, with header, footer and margins of appropriate size? (Remember that your supervisor may wish to hand write some annotations.)

- Created a title page? Is this your *exact* title as written in the **Mid-project Review** page of your Log?
- Included a contents page?
- Included a glossary of terms? This is not obligatory but for certain highly specialised or technical reports it can be a good idea.
- Numbered and named every page of your report?
- Ended your report with a word count? This is not obligatory but if you are writing a 5000-word report it demonstrates your achievement of this aim.
- Referenced *every* citation, diagram, photograph and image contained in your report?
- Created a reference list in the correct format for your chosen style of referencing?
- Included a bibliography, listing all sources used, including those not directly referenced in your report?
- Created, labelled and numbered appendices as appropriate for your EP?
- Checked all spellings and grammar by proofreading and/or using appropriate software?
- Collated your report pages and used either staples or treasury tags to hold them in the correct order?

 Example

Rose was delighted to have completed her EP. She was feeling rather pressured at college because she had fallen behind with her Biology homework. She printed out her report, straight from her laptop, and put the ten printed pages, unstapled, into one plastic poly pocket.

When her EP was read by her supervisor it was discovered that Rose's report did not appear to make sense. She had put the pages into the poly pocket in the wrong order. Rose had neither named nor numbered her loose report pages. Thus her materials were not 'appropriately presented' (see AQA criteria in Appendix 5).

What you must submit

The two items that *must* be submitted are a **completed Production Log** and an **EP report**.

If your product is an artefact you must either submit the artefact itself or submit sufficient evidence of the artefact so that its quality and fitness for purpose can be judged as well as photographic evidence of the different stages of production.

 Examples

Lucas created a board game to help young children learn Spanish. The board game itself was included in his EP submission, with all the loose parts carefully packaged.

Lily was a member of an EP group working on a social action project. Working with Amnesty International, the group planned and executed several awareness-raising campaign days in their local community. The evidence of this artefact EP that was submitted included:

- video footage of the group setting up their stalls in the town centre

TIP

The way you present your EP submission matters. It should be easy to handle and easy to read, with a 'logical and coherent structure' (see AQA criteria in Appendix 5).

- still photographs taken throughout the campaign (no children were photographed and permission was sought from any person who appeared in a photo)
- photographs of the posters they had created showing the different initial and final versions of the posters
- exact copies of the leaflets that were created and handed out
- a signed letter from the secretary of the local Amnesty International branch, who observed the campaigning and was able to evaluate its effectiveness
- anonymous but authenticated copies of the signed petitions that were then sent to the local Member of Parliament

Sunil designed and created a computer game for young teenagers. He used specialist software and knew that he would be unable to submit it as an accessible piece of software playable on someone else's computer.

Sunil therefore submitted the original and modified pages of code that he had written and the storyboards he had created for the game. He filmed the screen of his laptop when the game was being played by his testers. He edited various clips of film together and recorded himself talking through the main features of the game to use as a voiceover.

The evidence Sunil submitted in his Log and report clearly showed all his research and how this research had influenced the various design decisions. The evidence submitted in terms of the coding, storyboarding and the film showed that the finished artefact was clearly fit for its intended audience.

TIP

If you have created a film or recorded a piece of music as your artefact, use 'standard' software packages so that you can submit your video or audio recordings on a memory stick that will be playable on a computer without requiring specialist software.

Your supervisor will judge your EP by scrutinising the evidence that you submit. If you submit photographs of your artefact that are blurred or very small, it is unlikely that your EP material will be judged to be 'appropriately presented' (see AQA criteria in Appendix 5). You should carefully consider the quality of any video or photographic evidence of your product realisation before you include it in your EP submission.

Do not expect your supervisor to take photographs or films for you. The responsibility for submission of appropriate assessment evidence lies with you.

What you might submit

So now you know the minimum requirements for submission: your **Log**, your **report** and your **artefact** (if appropriate).

Sometimes, however, it is appropriate to submit carefully selected additional evidence. What else might you choose to submit?

Planning evidence

You need to clearly evidence your planning methods. This can be achieved by good use of your Log alone, but you might like to consider including some of the following as appendices:

- The concept maps that helped you find your topic (if you created any).
- Your planning documents (if you used a Gantt chart or action plan, etc.).
- An extract from your research journal/blog (if you used one).

For some artefact EPs, extracts of the storybook or sketchbook may offer good evidence of planning.

Primary data collection

If you undertook primary data collection it would be sensible to submit evidence of the raw primary data, or a summary of your primary data together with analysis, in an appendix.

Depending on what your primary research involved you may include some of the following in appendices:

- A single copy of your pilot questionnaire plus a single copy of the actual questionnaire you used, together with collated responses from your questionnaires, perhaps with graphical representations of the data.
- A copy of your pilot interview questions plus a copy of your revised interview questions together with transcripts of all interviews undertaken.
- Summarised qualitative data gathered from focus groups.
- Data gathered by any experiments you undertook, either as raw data or presented in summary form.
- Letters, printed e-mails and social media screenshots.
- Statistical tests and analysis.

Once in an appendix you can then reference these items clearly in your report.

Example

As part of her EP related to dairy farming in the UK, Kali collected data from dairy farmers while she was doing work experience with a vet. She was investigating the milk yield obtained from four different breeds of cow: Holstein-Friesian, Ayrshire, Jersey and Guernsey. Kali classified a daily milk yield below 20 litres per day as low, a yield between 20 and 25 litres as medium and a yield over 25 litres per day as high.

In her report Kali decided only to include a brief summary of her statistical procedures and her conclusion that milk yield is related to breed, and to cite and reference the relevant appendix. In her appendix she included a summary of her primary data and all her statistical analysis, as shown opposite.

I have assumed that the sample of cows is random and will carry out a χ^2 test for association between milk yield and breed of cow. My null hypothesis is 'Milk yield is independent of breed'.

Table showing observed data (O) on milk yield by breed of cow

Breed of cow	Low	Medium	High	Total
Holstein Friesian	4	5	12	21
Jersey	10	6	4	20
Guernsey	8	17	7	32
Ayrshire	5	20	7	32
Total	27	48	30	105

Expected frequencies (E)

Breed of cow	Low	Medium	High
Holstein Friesian	5.4	9.6	6
Jersey	5.14	9.14	5.71
Guernsey	8.23	14.63	9.14
Ayrshire	8.23	14.63	9.14

H_0 Milk yield is independent of breed.

H_1 Milk yield is not independent of breed.

Taking 1% level of significance:

Test statistic = $\sum \dfrac{(O - E)^2}{E}$ = 19.38 (calculated by me using values from the two tables)

χ^2 critical value for 6 degrees of freedom = 16.81 (from statistical tables)

19.38 > 16.81

So I can reject H_0 and conclude that there is evidence to suggest milk yield is not independent of breed.

Holstein Friesian dairy cows

Presentation evidence

Since you have put a lot of effort into preparing for and delivering your presentation, it might be a good idea to include more than just the evidence of planning as found in your Log, page 12, **Presentation Record Part A**.

You might consider including (if you used these):

- a printout of your PowerPoint slides, your Prezi 'path steps', or equivalent
- a photograph of your 'marketplace' stand
- your presentation notes or cue cards
- a photograph of your poster or possibly the poster itself
- a photograph of any props used at your presentation
- a copy of your presentation handout

Other possible additional evidence

If you have particular items relevant to your EP that need to be seen in order for their quality to be judged, you can include them in an appendix. For example:

- your risk assessment documentation
- your evaluation of your resources (you may prefer to submit this in an appendix if you have not integrated it into your Log or report)
- consent forms, debriefing notes or other materials used with any research participants
- adverts for your EP event and the event programme
- the catalogue for your exhibition
- letters of congratulations, thanks from members of your audience or beneficiaries of your product

TIP

Allow yourself plenty of time to put all your project evidence together. It will take longer than you might think.

Gregory Green
Leading Edge High School
Contemporary Way
Modchester
XX2 8LE

1st April 2020

Dear Gregory,

I am writing on behalf of the patients and staff of the Kindred Children's Hospice. How very generous of you to focus such a wonderful fundraising effort on benefiting the children who come to spend time in our care. We are going to use your money to develop a state of the art 'sensory garden' in the front courtyard to greatly enhance the positive experience the children receive at our hospice.
You must have worked extremely hard to raise such a fantastic sum! We greatly appreciate your efforts and you must come and visit the garden as soon as it is complete. You will always be a very welcome visitor here.

I acknowledge receipt of your cheque for £2423.

Yours sincerely,

Mortimer Jones

Mortimer Jones

Figure 9.1 A letter of thanks is a form of additional evidence

 Example

Liam, Pat and Thea worked together in a group to put on a talent show at their school.

Liam was responsible for publicity, budget and sponsorship. He designed the advertisements, one for the school's electronic newsletter and one A3-sized poster that was put up throughout the school. He also designed the tickets and the programme, both of which contained adverts from various local businesses that had agreed to sponsor the show. These items, in themselves, were not the artefact that was considered to be the group's 'product', but for Liam they provided relevant evidence of product realisation. The other members of the group did not include evidence of these items in their EP submissions.

What you should not submit

Sometimes students fail to notice the requirement for them to be **selective**. One of the skills that you need to develop is the ability to separate relevant and important evidence from unhelpful and irrelevant evidence.

Do not make the mistake of submitting a lever-arch file jam-packed with documents. Your submission, like your Log and your report, should be concise and focused.

Items that are *not* likely to be of value include:

- A video of your presentation — all presentation evidence submitted must be hard copy.
- Books — you should have learned how to create a bibliography and reference your resources.

- Leaflets — unless you are unable to reference them appropriately because there is no discernible publisher and so they cannot be reliably referenced.
- Highlighted printouts of online research that you have undertaken — you should have learned how to reference online resources.
- Dozens of completed questionnaires — one example is sufficient, together with a summary of your collected responses.
- Your research journal — perhaps photocopy one page as an example.
- A complete printout of your EP blog — perhaps include one extract printed out as an example.
- A Gantt chart printed out so that it spans multiple pages — if you decide to include a copy of your planning charts or documents, format them to fit easily on to one page.
- Irrelevant material, such as notes taken during your Taught Skills lessons, or research notes that refer to a different topic.
- Anything that has no label or heading.
- A scrapbook.

Remember that your project should have 'a logical and coherent structure' and that your project material should be 'consistently relevant, well-structured and appropriately presented' (see Appendix 5 for the AQA criteria).

Do *not*:

- submit your project materials in lever-arch or ring binder files
- use plastic poly-pockets

Do:

- label and name each section/item within your submission
- make sure that any submitted USBs, CDs or DVDs are firmly attached to your other documents

CHECKLIST

Questions that I need to consider:

- ☐ Is my Production Log completed and collated correctly?
- ☐ Is my report printed out legibly, with pages in the correct order and firmly attached?
- ☐ Have I included sufficient evidence of my artefact so that its quality can be accurately judged?
- ☐ Is my selected 'additional' evidence clearly labelled, organised and relevant?

Appendix 1

Risk assessment

This is not a requirement of the EPQ specification but it may be a requirement of your school or college. Put simply, undertaking a formal risk assessment of the proposed research elements of your EP will help you identify any associated risks so you can put in place 'control measures' to ensure that any risks are reduced to an acceptable level.

Your school or college may have a preferred style of risk assessment, but using a simple form like the one below should be sufficient for most EPs. A few examples from different scenarios have been included to help you consider potential risks involved with the EPQ and how they might be avoided.

If you are unable to reduce a risk to a level that is considered acceptable by your centre coordinator, it is unlikely that your proposal will be approved.

Table 1 Extended Project risk assessment

Name:		Project focus:		
Activity	**Hazard**	**Who is at risk?**	**What am I doing to reduce the risk? (Control measures)**	**Is the risk now low?**
Travelling to the university library	Road traffic accident	Me	Travel using public transport Only cross roads at crossings with traffic lights	Yes
Tasting my energy bars	Food poisoning	The volunteer tasters	Closely follow food hygiene advice from the FSA	Yes
Collecting heather samples on moor	Injury or becoming lost	Me	Ask two friends to come with me In case of accident we then have 'one to stay and one to seek help'	Yes
Building my robot	Failing to complete the build in time to submit	Me	Detailed research including contact with robot builders so that my design is one that can be built in time In planning I will build in plenty of time for testing/improving	Yes
Working together in a group	Failing to keep in close contact, not noticing that one group member has 'given up'	The whole group	Using project management software such as that offered by www.smartsheet.com to keep fully in touch with group members' EP activities	Yes

Appendix 2

The ethics of research

If you decide that your EP would benefit from some research that involves human beings or animals in any way, you should fully consider the ethics related to your research. Put simply, your research should not be **harmful**. Harm can come from many directions and does not refer simply to physical harm. No EPQ research should be undertaken that might result in either the physical or psychological harm of research participants. It is also important that you do not embark on research that might be harmful to *you*. For example, if you interview people unknown to you, it would be unwise to go alone. There are many potential resources to which exposure could be harmful to you. (See Appendix 1 for the use of **risk assessment** to identify and reduce the risk of harm.)

Human beings

If you intend to use interviews, questionnaires or experiments with human research participants you should consider all of the following before embarking:

- Have you sought permission from the participants in such a way that they understand what is being asked of them? This is called '**informed consent**'. Note that for EPQ students it is essential that you do not attempt an experiment where deliberate deception of participants is involved.
- Have you made it clear to participants that they have the '**right to withdraw**' from your research at any time, even if they have previously given consent?
- Have you fully discussed **confidentiality**? That is, that you will make every effort to keep the data you collect safe and you will not share it with anyone else.
- Have you fully discussed **anonymity**? You should be able to assure your research participants that every effort will be made by you to ensure that the data they provide cannot be traced back to them in your project submission, including your Log, report and presentation, unless they have given permission to be identified.

Many interviewees prefer to remain anonymous, but experts in a particular field may be happy to be identified. In such cases you must explain clearly to them:

- how the information they supply will be used
- how, if at all, they will be identified
- how, and for how long, the information will be stored
- who will see the information
- whether there might be any onward transmission of the information

You should produce, and have approved by your supervisor, appropriate documents:

- **Signed consent** from participants, but note that if a child is under 18 then they cannot legally give consent themselves and you must ask a parent or guardian for consent. Think very carefully before involving any under-18-year-olds in your research. If this research is intended to take place in a school setting, consent must also be obtained from the headteacher.
- A **briefing sheet** to use with participants before commencing the data collection exercise. This should provide brief and clear information on the key elements of your research: what it is about, the voluntary nature of participant involvement, what will happen during and after the research has taken place.
- A **debriefing sheet** to use with participants after the data has been collected. Thank the participants for their involvement, outline the background to your research (including your aims, measurements or observations, and hypotheses), remind participants how you intend to store your data (and that it will be kept anonymous and confidential), repeat the right of participants to withdraw any/all of the data collected from them without giving you a reason. You should also provide contact details for your supervisor.
- Precise **details** of any questionnaires, interview questions or experimental procedures that you intend to use, together with a full assessment of these for their potential to harm the participants. You must show clearly how you have reduced any potential harm to a level that is no greater than that experienced by your research participants in their everyday life.

Animals

The Nuffield Council on Bioethics published a report entitled 'The ethics of research involving animals' that discusses the complex ethical issues relating to research involving animals. For your EP it is important that you do not undertake any research involving animals that might cause suffering to the animals.

Appendix 3

Analysis of data

Whether your EP includes data collected by others or primary data collected by you, it is likely that at some point within your EP you will find yourself displaying, describing or analysing data of some sort. This appendix will not provide you with a complete course in data display and analysis, but it will offer you some suggestions.

Whether you use secondary data collected by others or primary data collected by you, many of the decisions that you need to make will be similar.

When looking at data you should assess both the data and its analysis in terms of:

- **Validity:** Is it accurate and does it genuinely represent what it claims to represent? Ask yourself questions such as: Were my respondents truthful? Were all my measurements checked?
- **Reliability:** Would another researcher conducting very similar research produce more or less the same result?
- **Representativeness:** Was an appropriate sample size and sampling technique used so that this sample can truly be said to represent the targeted population?

Collecting data

Imagine that you have decided that data collection via some kind of survey or experiment would be of value to your EP. You need to decide how much data to collect and how it relates to the 'parent population' under investigation. If the population is small, for example the members of your immediate family, you will not need to take a sample as you can collect data from every member of the population — this is called a 'census'.

In the UK, for example, census data is gathered from every household every ten years. This data is more reliable than taking samples in terms of gaining a true picture relating to the characteristics of the population. Making use of UK census data can be a sensible decision for some EP students. The data collection has been done for you.

If a population is large, however, taking a census yourself becomes impractical. Usually the best that can be done by an EP student is to take a sample from the population under investigation.

Choosing a sample

First of all you need to clearly define your **population**. In statistics the term 'population' does not always refer to living beings. For example, you might be studying the weights of male Siamese cats. In this case the population will be the set of *weights* of all the male Siamese cats in the world, not the cats themselves.

You also need to decide which variable(s) you are interested in. A **variable** is any characteristic, number or quantity that can be measured or counted. Age, gender, favourite colour, length of bean pod, eye colour and blood pressure are examples of variables.

Once the population and variable(s) are clearly defined you need to select a sample. For your data to produce results from which you can draw meaningful conclusions, you should consider carefully how big your **sample size** should be. What sample size is suitable will depend on the type of data you are collecting. There are free sample size calculators available online, for example SurveyMonkey has a 'Calculating the number of respondents you need' tool. This helps you calculate a suitable sample size if you intend to statistically analyse quantitative data. For qualitative data the sample size depends on having sufficient responses to reach 'saturation', i.e. the point where additional responses won't provide any additional insights.

Many different sorts of sampling are used by researchers. Note, however, that most statistical testing that you might want to undertake requires that your sample is **random**. What this means, put simply, is that every member of a population has an equal chance of being selected and placed into the sample. In practice, random sampling is difficult to achieve and may not be possible because researchers have insufficient time or resources.

If you intend to take samples in order to gather data, you should investigate possible methods carefully before deciding on the **sampling method** that you will choose. Each type of sampling that might be used has advantages and disadvantages:

- **Simple random:** Can only be used where every member of the population can be identified. One method would be to allocate to every member of a population a raffle ticket, put the tickets into a hat, shake them up and pull the required number of tickets out of the hat. This is the ideal form of sampling but in many situations it is impossible to identify every member of a population.
- **Systematic:** Again, this can only be used when every member of a population is identifiable and can be listed. From the list you can choose, say, every twentieth individual.
- **Stratified:** When a population has clearly defined different groups or 'strata', for example year groups at a school. To ensure that each year group is fairly represented a randomly selected number of students from each group would be included, in proportion to the size of the group.
- **Opportunity:** This form of sampling is not random. It might mean using the first members of the population encountered for the sample. For example, when sampling bean pods in a large bean field, take your whole sample of bean pods near to the gate where you entered the field.
- **Quota:** This is a non-random form of stratified sampling. Each stratum is represented in correct proportion, but the sample within the stratum is chosen by opportunity.
- **Snowball:** This form of sampling can be of use to investigate very specialised, difficult-to-reach populations, for example canvassing the opinions of left-handed tennis players. In your local region there is probably no register of left-handed players, however it is quite likely that one left-handed player can recommend another, from having played tennis with them.
- **Volunteer:** This form of sampling occurs when you advertise your need for participants and choose your sample from participants who respond to your advert. This could be as simple as standing up in a school assembly and saying that you are looking for some fans of Harry Styles to help you with your EP research.

Once you have selected a sample it might be helpful to use a set of pie charts to demonstrate various characteristics of your selected sample.

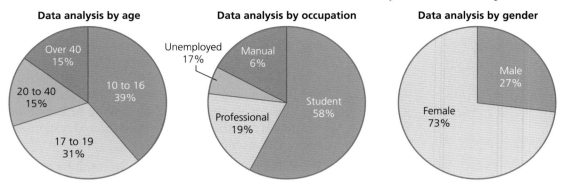

Figure 10.1 Pie charts showing characteristics of a sample

🔍 Example

Joel wants to conduct a survey to establish local opinions about a proposed major new shopping centre. Questions he must ask himself include:

- How do I define my population? What constitutes 'local'? People who live within a 5 km radius of the shopping centre? People who spend their working week within this radius, at school or work, but who live elsewhere?
- How big should my sample be?
- How could I select my sample?
- Will this sample fairly represent the entire local population?
- Have fair proportions of different population 'strata' been selected?
- Am I justified in generalising my results and making predictions about the opinions of those who were not included in the survey?

Quantitative data analysis

Once you have selected your sample and collected your data, what do you do with it?

The first thing to note here is that **statistical** analysis of data collected for your EP will require more than the drawing of a few graphs and charts if you want to use your data in any meaningful way. You will need to decide which, if any, of the possible numerical measures — mean, median, mode, percentiles, quartiles, range, variance, standard deviation — are appropriate values to evaluate.

Having found one or more of these measures you then need to **interpret** the measures. What do these values allow you to say about your sample? What can you infer about the population, if anything? Are you using them to make comparisons between two different populations?

> **TIP**
>
> Always look carefully at your results before including them in your report. For example, using percentages is not always appropriate unless you are comparing samples of different sizes. If you are taking snapshots of opinion and your sample size is 11, do not say, for example, 'Of the sample, 27.3% agreed that...', say 'Three out of the 11 participants agreed...'

This book cannot provide you with full guidance and teaching related to statistical procedures, but here is some guidance so that you can research the techniques most appropriate for your data.

Before you decide to collect any **quantitative** (measured or counted) data you should think carefully about what analysis you can carry out.

First, decide if your data is **discrete** (stepped or counted) or **continuous** (measured, e.g. using scales, a timer or a tape measure). For example:

- Shoe sizes are discrete — they can be 36, 37, 38, 39, etc., but there is no sense in saying shoe size 39.2.
  The length of a person's foot is continuous — you can measure to whatever accuracy you choose: to the nearest centimetre, to the nearest millimetre, etc.
- Women's dress sizes are discrete — 6, 8, 10, 12, 14, etc.
  Women's heights are continuous.
- The number of lambs in a field is discrete.
  The weight of a lamb is continuous.

Example

Faye is comparing the heights of pea plants grown in different conditions.

The pea plants germinated at the same time, grew in the same compost and in the same sized pots. The freshly germinated plants were subjected to the same light intensity and given the same daily quantity of water. Faye created four sets of plants, each comprised 30 pea plants and was kept at one of four different constant temperatures.

Faye was interested to see if temperature affected the height of the pea plants.

Faye measured the height of each plant at the end of the week for four successive weeks. She collected data from the four different populations that could be compared and analysed.

Discrete data

The most commonly used **numerical measures** of quantitative data are the mean, median, mode, range and standard deviation.

In many cases EPQ students have just one set of discrete data taken from the population under consideration. You might, however, want to investigate an association between two discrete variables.

 Example

Susan wanted to investigate whether there was an association between gender and preferred form of reading.

She gathered data from a random sample of boys and girls in her sixth form and asked one simple question:

Do you prefer reading on a tablet, or do you prefer reading a book?

Her two variables are gender and preferred form of reading.

Preferred form of reading	Male	Female	Total
Tablet	24	30	54
Book	15	21	36
Total	39	51	90

If you are seeking to determine whether a **correlation** exists, the data must be 'paired'. Each set of data must have the same number of data points and each data point in one set of data must be related to one, and only one, data point in the other data set. In some cases this pairing might exist because two measurements correspond to the same person.

 Example

Toby wanted to see if a correlation existed between the number of ice creams eaten and the number of fizzy drinks consumed by students in Year 12 at his school.

He gathered data from students in Year 12, with students identified by number only.

Toby collected paired data for 50 students. One data set gave the numbers of ice creams eaten by each student in a specified week, while the other data set gave the corresponding numbers of cans of fizzy drink consumed.

You must decide which one of the situations described in the table opposite fits the discrete data that you intend to collect/have collected. The possible analyses/tests that you might then use are listed.

Note that these statistical tests are designed for use with **random** samples.

Table 2 Analyses and tests for discrete data

For one set of data	For one set of data, where an association is to be investigated	To compare two sets of data	To compare two sets of data	To compare three or more sets of data
Numerical measures can be evaluated	You must be able to divide the data between two distinct variables	Where the data is presented as one set of **matched pairs**	Where the data is presented as two **separate independent sets**	Numerical measures can be evaluated for each set of data
A box plot, a bar chart and/or a line diagram can be drawn	You need to collect sufficient data so that no 'cell' (entry in a contingency table) contains a frequency less than 5	Correlation can be investigated using **Spearman's rank correlation coefficient** (SRCC)	Numerical measures can be evaluated for each sample	Multiple bar charts or line diagrams can be drawn
A **sign test** for a population median can be used A **Wilcoxon signed-rank test** for a population median or mean can be used, provided the data is symmetrically distributed	A χ^2 **test** (chi-squared test) for association can be used	A scatter diagram can be drawn	A dual bar chart or line diagram can be drawn	A **Kruskal-Wallis test** can be undertaken
		A **sign test** for the difference in population medians can be used A **Wilcoxon signed-rank test** for a difference in the population medians or the means can be used, provided the differences are symmetrically distributed	A **Mann-Whitney U** (Wilcoxon rank sum) test for difference in population medians can be used	

TIP

There are many data analysis software packages available for quantitative data. Many EP students use sites such as SurveyMonkey to both gather and display data, while others develop their skills in using Microsoft Excel.

Continuous data

Data collected by students of the EPQ is frequently continuous if it has come from some form of experiment. For example:

- Depth of water
- Time taken to travel from home to school
- Weight of pebbles
- Temperature of fermenting compost

You must decide which one of the situations described in the table on page 138 fits the **continuous data** that you intend to or have collected. The possible analyses/tests that you might then use are listed.

This table contains terminology that you may not be familiar with:

- σ is the standard deviation of the parent population.
- data $\sim N$ indicates that data is normally distributed.
- z-test means that the normal distribution is used for the test.
- t-test indicates that a t-distribution is used for the test.

Note that these statistical tests are designed for use with **random** samples.

Table 3 Analyses and tests for continuous data

One set of data has been collected	One set of data has been collected	One set of data has been collected	Two sets of data have been collected	Two sets of data have been collected	Three or more sets of data have been collected
Small set of data (fewer than 30 in sample)	**Small set of data** (fewer than 30 in sample)	**Large set of data** (more than 30 in sample)	Two sets of data to be compared	Two sets of data to be compared	Three or more sets of data to be compared
Numerical measures can be evaluated	Numerical measures can be evaluated	Numerical measures can be evaluated	Where the data is presented as one set of **matched pairs**	Where the data is presented as two **separate independent sets**	
A box plot, a histogram and/or a cumulative frequency curve can be drawn	A box plot, a histogram and/or a cumulative frequency curve can be drawn	A box plot, a histogram and/or a cumulative frequency curve can be drawn	Correlation can be investigated using the **Pearson product-moment correlation coefficient** (PMCC)	Numerical measures can be evaluated for each sample	An **analysis of variance** (ANOVA) can be undertaken
σ **known**	σ **not known**	σ **known or not known**	A scatter diagram can be drawn	A dual bar chart and/or a line diagram can be drawn	
You can use a **z-test** for the population mean, assuming data $\sim N$	You can use a **t-test** for the population mean, assuming data $\sim N$	You can use a **z-test** for the population mean, assuming data $\sim N$	You can use a *t*-test for difference in population means provided σ known and data $\sim N$	A **z-test** for the means can be undertaken, provided σ known and data $\sim N$ A **t-test** for the means can be undertaken, where σ not known provided data $\sim N$	

Qualitative data analysis

How should you analyse non-numeric data? Analysis of qualitative data can be very time-consuming. You must give *every* opinion and idea a fair reading, even when you personally disagree with it. You are trying to impose order on your collected data and to identify the dominant ideas within the data. You may undertake thematic, content or conversational analysis.

- If you have some **open questions** in a questionnaire or interview, or if you are gathering expert opinions from a range of sources, you need to seek out repeated themes/ideas/responses.
- If you decide to use **focus groups** to gather data then use groups of between five and eight participants and encourage interaction between the participants. This may lead to agreement/disagreement on key issues.
- If you have used a **case study** remember that you should not use this to generalise — there could be unique properties of this particular person/place/situation. (The same caution should be applied to all analysis of qualitative data.)

Word clouds are one way to help you with the analysis of qualitative data. If you input all the open responses into a word cloud generator, such as Wordle, the most frequently occurring words will be immediately obvious. Be aware, however, that different people may use different words to express similar ideas. Your analysis should be more concerned with the ideas behind any words used, rather than the words themselves.

Example

Robyn was investigating opinions held by boys and by girls attending her school regarding the food that is available to buy at the school cafeteria. This was part of Robyn's EP that had as its aim the development of an improved take-up of 'healthy eating' options by the students at her school.

In a questionnaire completed by equal numbers of randomly selected boys and randomly selected girls from each of the seven year groups attending her school, one of her open questions asked:

If you could change just one thing about the menu of the school cafeteria, what would it be?

Robyn copied all the free responses from the girl respondents and then all the free responses from the boys separately into Wordle, so she could see what the key hoped-for changes were and whether there were any interesting differences between boys and girls.

TIP

If you want to analyse a significant quantity of qualitative data you might like to use the free version of http://atlasti.com. This is a computer program used by researchers working with qualitative data and its subsequent analysis.

Appendix 4

Resources

This is a non-exhaustive alphabetical list of possible resources that could be used as you undertake the EPQ, depending on your chosen topic.

- Acts of Parliament
- Advertisements (used to spot gender stereotyping in twentieth-century Britain, for example)
- Apps (for example a planning app to help with your project management)
- Archives
- Art galleries
- Authors
- Blogs (but make sure the identity of the blogger is known)
- Books
- Buildings (especially if your EP relates to engineering/architecture)
- Cartoons (historical cartoons can show a great deal about public opinion, for example)
- Census data
- Charities
- Concerts
- Conversations (do not forget to provide transcript evidence of these)
- Debates
- E-mails (include a printed copy in an appendix)
- Encyclopedias
- Experiments (both your own and those of others)
- Experts
- Facebook
- Family holidays (the opportunity to visit relevant places for your EP, to collect primary data)
- Field trips
- Films
- Focus groups
- Geological surveys
- Google Earth/Maps
- Government publications
- Graphs and charts (but make sure that you understand what they show and that you can communicate this in your report)
- Hansard (edited verbatim report of proceedings of both the House of Commons and the House of Lords)
- Historical works (both fiction and non-fiction)
- Images ('a picture speaks a thousand words')
- Internships and holiday placements
- Interviews (do not forget to provide transcript evidence of these)
- iPlayer (for the relevant television programme that you found out about too late to watch live)
- Journals (both print and electronic)
- Judges (particular legal rulings can be highly significant)
- Law reports
- Lectures (take careful notes)
- Lyrics to songs
- Magazines
- Materials (from which to create your artefact)
- Measuring devices
- Mobile phones (a very useful resource, use yours perhaps to take photos, record interviews, write notes, access your calendar and/or check out facts via the internet)
- Museums
- Music
- Newspapers
- Ordnance Survey maps
- Paintings
- People
- Pinterest
- Podcasts
- Poetry
- Politicians
- Posters
- Questionnaires
- Radio programmes
- Religious texts
- Scientific information (from books, journals, laboratories, experts)
- Sculpture
- Social media
- Sporting venues/occasions/technology
- Statutes
- Surveys
- Television programmes (documentaries, televised theatrical productions, political debates, news footage, etc.)
- Text messages (keep copies)
- Theatre
- Tools (used to create your artefact)
- Translation software (such as Google Translate, for information found in a foreign language)
- Twitter
- Universities
- Unpublished works (must still be referenced)
- Videos
- Wikipedia
- Work experience (expert interviews/specialist equipment)
- YouTube

Appendix 5

AQA criteria

Your supervisor will judge your EP. There are four aspects of this judgement:

AO1	**Manage:** Identify, design, plan and carry out a project, applying a range of skills, strategies and methods to achieve objectives.
AO2	**Use resources:** Research, critically select, organise and use information, and select and use a range of resources. Analyse data. Apply relevantly and demonstrate understanding of any links, connections and complexities of the topic.
AO3	**Develop and realise:** Select and use a range of skills, including, where appropriate, new technologies and problem-solving, to take decisions critically and achieve planned outcomes.
AO4	**Review:** Evaluate all aspects of the Extended Project, including outcomes in relation to stated objectives and own learning and performance. Select and use a range of communication skills and media to present evidenced project outcomes and conclusions in an appropriate format.

The following criteria are used to judge your project as fitting into one of three bands, depending on the evidence that you have submitted: top, middle or lower.

AO1 Manage

- Identify the topic
- Identify project aims and objectives
- Produce a Project Plan
- Complete the work, applying organisational skills and strategies to meet stated objectives

AQA criteria

- **Top:** Clear identification of the topic to be investigated or researched and clear evidence of appropriate aims and objectives for the proposed project title.
  Detailed Project Plan, with clear evidence of monitoring progress of project work against the agreed objectives.
- **Middle:** Some identification of the topic to be investigated or researched and some evidence of appropriate aims and objectives for the proposed project title.
  Project Plan with some evidence of monitoring progress of project work against the agreed objectives.
- **Lower:** Limited identification of the topic to be investigated or researched and limited evidence of appropriate aims and objectives for the proposed project title.
  Brief Project Plan, with little evidence of monitoring progress of project work against the agreed objectives.

AO2 Use resources

- Obtain and select from a variety of resources
- Analyse data
- Apply information relevantly
- Demonstrate understanding of appropriate links

AQA criteria

- **Top:** Evidence of detailed research involving the selection and evaluation of a wide range of relevant resources.
  Critical analysis and application of the resources with clear links made to appropriate theories and concepts.
- **Middle:** Evidence of some research involving the selection and evaluation of a range of relevant resources.
  Some analysis and application of the research, with links made to appropriate theories and concepts.
- **Lower:** Evidence of limited research involving limited selection and evaluation of resources.
  Little or no analysis and application of the resources, with few links made to appropriate theories and concepts.

AO3 Develop and realise

- Problem-solving
- Decision-making
- Creative thinking
- Achieve planned outcomes

AQA criteria

- **Top:** Candidates take appropriate decisions and appropriate data is collected and thoroughly analysed. The Project Plan is fully implemented and the outcome is fully realised to a high standard and consistent with the candidate's finally agreed plan.
  There is clear evidence of appropriate changes to or development of the initial Project Plan or title or aims and objectives, with clear and appropriate reasons for any changes.
  Candidates communicate their findings fluently in an appropriate format, synthesising information from a variety of sources, and present them within a logical and coherent structure that addresses closely the nature of the task.
- **Middle:** Candidates take decisions and some appropriate data is collected and adequately analysed. The Project Plan is implemented and the outcome is sufficiently realised to an acceptable standard and consistent with the candidate's finally agreed plan.
  There is some evidence of appropriate changes to or development of the initial Project Plan or title or aims and objectives, with reasons for any changes.
  Candidates communicate clearly their findings, showing some ability to synthesise information from different sources and present it in a structured manner appropriate to the task.
- **Lower:** Candidates take few decisions and a little data is insufficiently analysed. The Project Plan is implemented in a limited way and the outcome is realised in a limited manner not always consistent with the candidate's finally agreed plan.

There is little or no evidence of appropriate changes to or development of the initial Project Plan or title or aims and objectives, with only limited reasons for any changes.

Candidates communicate their findings by drawing on a limited number of sources and present them in a manner not always appropriate to the task.

AO4 Review

- Communication skills
- Convey and present evidenced outcomes and conclusions
- Evaluate own learning and performance

AQA criteria

- **Top:** Detailed and careful evaluation of the strengths and weaknesses of the completed project in relation to the planning, implementation and outcomes, and the candidate's own learning during the project. Material is consistently relevant, well-structured and appropriately presented. Candidates clearly communicate their findings and conclusions, which are based on sound evidence and judgement.
- **Middle:** Some evaluation of the strengths and weaknesses of the completed project in relation to the planning, implementation and outcomes, and the candidate's own learning during the project. Material is sometimes relevant, well-structured and appropriately presented. Candidates communicate their findings and conclusions, which are based on some evidence and judgement.
- **Lower:** Limited evaluation of the strengths and weaknesses of the completed project in relation to the planning, implementation and outcomes, and the candidate's own learning during the project. Material is not always relevant, well-structured or appropriately presented. Candidates communicate some of their findings and conclusions, which are based on little or no evidence and judgement.

Please refer to the AQA Extended Project Qualification specification as your definitive source of information.

Index

V

validity 132
variables 132–33
vested interest 58
video/film
  embedding into presentation slides 99, 111
  as part of artefact report 84
  submitting as evidence 123
visual aids, presentation tool 101–02
viva-style presentations 98
volunteer sampling 133

W

websites for research 55–56
whiteboards, digital, planning tool 29, 72
Wikipedia 53

Wilcoxon signed-rank test 137
word clouds 96–97, 138
word total 7, 16, 19, 83
  artefact reports 7, 83
  drafting and redrafting report 88
  end report with word count 88, 122
working title 16
  aims and objectives 20
  errors in choosing 16–19
  finalising 77–78
  SMART objectives 29
  successful 78–81
  writing of report *see* report writing
written resources, evaluation of 56–63

Z

z-test 138